CW00486768

The Man
Who Loved
Angels

Anthony Strano

BRAHMA KUMARIS

BKIS

Original text by Anthony Strano
Edited by John McConnel & Judy Johnson

Copyright © 2016 BKIS Publications, London

PRINT ISBN   978-1-886872-27-1
KINDLE ISBN   978-1-886872-30-1
EPUB ISBN   978-1-886872-33-2

First published in 2016 by Brahma Kumaris Information Services Ltd,
Global Co-operation House, 65 Pound Lane, London, NW10 2HH
Website: www.inspiredstillness.com
E-mail: hello@lnspiredstillness.com

The right of Anthony Strano to be identified as the Author of the Work has been
asserted by him in accordance with the Copyright, Designs and Patents Act 1988.

All rights reserved. No part of this book may be reproduced by any mechanical,
photographic or electronic process, or in the form of a photographic or audio
recording, or stored in a retrieval system, transmitted or otherwise copied for
public or private use without the written permission of the publisher. Requests for
permission should be addressed to: BK Publications, Global Co-operation House,
65 Pound Lane, London, NW10 2HH

PUBLISHER'S NOTE

The Publishers would like to acknowledge that Julie Beacall shared the idea of
a book she was working on about an Apprentice Angel in 2008 with us at BK
Publications. Anthony Strano then worked on a book of the same title, later
calling it 'The 'Making of an Angel'.

We look forward to the publication of Julie's original concept in the near future.

Cover designed by Judi Rich
Designed by Samir Patra
Printed in India by Imprint Press.

This book is produced using acid-free paper from registered
sustainable and managed sources.

We shall find peace.
We shall hear angels. We shall see the
sky sparkling with diamonds.

Anton Chekhov

Also by Anthony Strano

BOOKS
Discovering Spirituality
Remember
Reflections - For Dawn, Day & Dusk
The Alpha Point
Seeking Silence
The Quest for Well-Being
Slaying the Three Dragons

AUDIO CDs
8 Principles of Spirituality
A Time for Healing
Creating a Hero
Link of Life
Embracing Forgiveness
Just-a-Minute CD 2

PREFACE ON ANGELS

Angels are beings of pure light and love

As the first and direct creation of God, angels have an easy and constant link with the Divine.

Being aware that they belong to 'the One', they never forget their responsibility towards other souls.

Angels go beyond limitations and conflict; their elevated consciousness and deep desire to care for others makes them fearless protectors.

They spread powerful vibrations of love and regard that enable others to recognise their own goodness and draw closer to God.

Whilst living in the world they remain pure, untouched by the gross or the mundane. Their treasure-store of positive feelings and good wishes is a hidden power that equips them to face any situation and transform it.

Angels value and enhance unity in any gathering. They comfort souls who may be sad, moody or confused and make them light.

In their presence, others are able to forgive and stop hurting each other.

They understand everyone and everything with ease and, as ambassadors of peace, they resolve conflicts between people by reminding them of each other's goodness.

Being aware that they are instruments in God's hands, they never act from a desire for support, recognition, or reward.

Having no ulterior motive, their love for God and service is unconditional, which is why they never tire.

The words of angels are filled with truth, respect and love and have the power to shape another's fortune and future.

Every word they speak is considered a blessing.

Angels are never surprised by the actions of another or by life's sudden scenes.

A deep love and faith in goodness enables them to help as much as is required and to become an inspiration for positive transformation.

Through their eyes, God showers His compassion and love on all.

Whoever receives a glance from an angel experiences a gentle yet empowering feeling of love.

Angels come in all sorts of guises. Each of us has the capacity to become an angel.

In remembrance of the One

B. K. Janki

Dadi Janki
Administrative Head of the Brahma Kumaris

AUTHOR'S INTRODUCTION

I remember once, when I was in India, being asked, "Are you going to call out to angels, or are you going to be an angel?"

This book is about the making of an angel.

I have always been fascinated by angels and spent many happy times thinking and talking about them and appreciating images of them. Several years ago a friend and I went to Italy and visited numerous churches, museums and art galleries in Milan, Rome etc. Seeing so many paintings and statues of angels, I wondered whether at one time an army (or was it a choir?) of angels had visited Italy. With so many paintings and statues of angels everywhere something must have happened. Some memory is surely recorded in all this art?

Having a deep love for angels and a belief that we all have within us the possibility of becoming an angel, I felt inspired to write this book about a youth called Michael, who is unexpectedly offered an apprenticeship with God to become an angel.

The text takes the form of:

1. The story of Michael which is divided into two parts; his experience as an apprentice in the school for angels and his first challenges after graduation.

2. A journal of the things Michael learned during his time at the school, which is offered to you, the reader, as a manual on how to become an angel. It includes reflections, awareness exercises and spiritual insights.

I hope that you will find the book of interest and that it will empower you to become an angel or, at least, appreciate the important role that angels can play in your life.

Anthony Strano, Greece 2014

EDITOR'S NOTE

Michael's transformation from a human being to an angel did not happen over night. He attended a school for angels for fourteen years where he was taught by Lady Aditi and other enlightened beings, including the Great Lord.

Michael's story in some ways mirrors that of Anthony's. Anthony was of Italian descent and brought up in Australia by loving parents on a farm where he developed a deep love for Nature and God. He was a Catholic and quite devout but he felt God was surrounded in mystery and that he did not really know Him.

In his early twenties Anthony spread his wings and went on a spiritual search which took him to India and then London. There in a small flat in a poor part of London, he found the equivalent of Lady Aditi, a powerful yogi called Dadi Janki.

Dadi Janki is one of the original students and leaders of the Brahma Kumaris. She was sent to the UK in the early 1970s to help spread the universal message of peace, love and self-transformation to the Western world.

The Brahma Kumaris has been described as 'a school for angels'. Part of its mission is to bring together and train a group of powerful souls who, through their dharna and loving vibrations, are able to reveal the true nature of God and inspire every soul to realise its true potential.

How is this achieved? By..

- Studying specific spiritual knowledge which clarifies the true nature of the self and of God, creates greater self awareness and gives more meaning, value and purpose to life on this Earth.

- Tapping into the essential peaceful nature of the soul and connecting with the Divine through the regular practice of Raja Yoga meditation. This connection strengthens the soul and gives it the power to overcome adversity and live a life of contentment.

- Walking the talk i.e. living a simple, pure lifestyle which supports the well-being of the soul. This includes eating vegetarian food and refraining from activities that could distract or disturb the soul.

- Serving humanity and Nature by freely sharing spiritual knowledge and working with others to create a better world in which all living beings can happily live together in peace and harmony.

Anthony was immediately attracted by the teachings and practices of the Brahma Kumaris and soon became a regular and committed student. He had found his spiritual home and was soon off on his travels again, this time as a spiritual teacher and an angel in training. He regularly made trips to the headquarters of the Brahma Kumaris in Mount Abu, Rajasthan, where he had many powerful, transformative experiences and developed a very deep connection with God whom he grew to know and love as a living Being of Truth, great humility and compassion.

Anthony became a much loved and respected teacher, student, friend and companion. He was very drawn to angels and strove to bring the qualities of an angel into all his interactions. He was well qualified to talk and write about angels because he was like an angel.

How he and Michael became angelic is revealed in his final writings. Unfortunately, Anthony passed away before being able to complete the book.

This compilation is offered as a lasting tribute to the man who loved angels.

CONTENTS

ANTHONY'S THOUGHTS
ON ANGELS

What is an angel? What does the CV of an angel read like? Because they do exist! We are living at a time of crossroads – economically, politically, socially and environmentally – but even now the human spirit can exist beyond such crises. We must look within ourselves; there are no solutions outside of us. There are many plans and programmes but no solutions.

The first step in becoming an angel is to meet my soul-self.

Until I am aware that I am a spiritual being, I can never be a human being. Angels, they say, are created from the pure thought of God. And, yes, human beings can become angels, just as they can become devils. But let's stay positive and optimistic.

In English there are three words for change: "change", "transformation" and "metamorphosis". The latter comes from the Greek and means "complete transformation", like from a caterpillar to a butterfly.

When a human soul responds with generosity and compassion to the earth, then metamorphosis begins. Such souls move away from their small selves and lose their trivial problems as they let eternity into their hearts.

Once I let eternity into my heart, I will feel that all humanity is my family. And once my heart is unlimited, I become an angel.

What comes between the caterpillar and the butterfly? The cocoon. So I have to cocoon myself away from the eyes of others to respond to the needs of the moment. Then that deep metamorphosis quietly takes place. A cocoon is made of threads. Three threads weave the cocoon of spiritual transformation: *silence, knowledge and love.*

There are some human souls that have that type of love; one of their characteristics is being able to catch the current of divine love. They become totally focused on that. They serve other people's sorrow, but never get entangled in it. They never use compassion or mercy in the wrong way. They never try to play the saviour; they are just instruments of divine love and divine light.

What keeps the metamorphosis going? What keeps the cocoon working?

Introspection – always making sure that the link with the divine source is flowing. Because right now we need another energy and another consciousness.

Many people at the moment feel a kind of poison inside and are calling out to God. But they are also calling out to the closest companions of God, angels.

Angels are universal. They don't have a religion – they are not Christians or Hindus and neither are they Muslims. They are just pure beings. And the whole of humanity is their family. They don't just know it, they feel and act on it.

Angels are very loving but also very detached. They are never pulled in by the gravity of problems. They help souls to solve problems but will not be drawn in themselves because they have to keep wise when serving. If they were to get sick or polluted themselves, then how could they help others? A real angel will never be made sick by their ego, attachments, wrong motives, or by getting too involved in the small details and failing to see the bigger picture.

People hear angels and they are feeling their presence more and more. This is one way that angels serve – by their presence; they don't have to speak. They display a very special movement; they appear and disappear. But when they appear, even just for a second, people feel the presence of God and sense great hope. Because angels are messengers, they bring the message of God's love. They are protectors, able to protect the human soul against itself. We don't need protection from others as much as we need it from ourselves.

An angel is also a guide, saying "Don't go that way" or "Don't have that thought or feeling". The angel says, "Look where you are. You are stuck. Don't you want to change?" The angel is also a healer, bestowing on us his or her own good feelings, attitudes and virtues. For example, their patience heals anger and their stability heals mistrust.

When a person is stable and anchored, others can trust him or her. So an angel teaches the human how to heal, saying, "Have such *self-respect* that you don't need to compare yourself to anybody anymore. Have such *lightness* that you never get bitter. Have such *generosity* that you never need to think or speak of the weaknesses of others. Have such *understanding* that you can make the past the past. And have such *humility* that you can learn from everything and never become a victim."

The angel will whisper all this to you. We can get this directly from God if we are strong enough, but sometimes we are not very well tuned in, and it is then that an angel helps. This is how an angel heals.

An angel is a bridge between time and eternity, between humanity and God, between the old and the new – an angel is a point of intersection, forming a real bridge that many can cross over.

How will an angel help you then?

Firstly an angel will put a thought in your mind, "Remember who you are, your value and your original dignity. Never forget what you are in terms of eternity. You are a soul who is loved by the universe – do you remember?"

God tells us all this too, but sometimes we are unable to hear or understand Him. The angel just repeats what God is saying: "Remember who you are." Problems begin when we forget who we are; we identify instead with roles and try to live through other people, sabotaging every part of our lives. "Stop! Stop!" says the angel.

Secondly an angel will plant in your mind the thought that God is love; He is pure and kind, without any form of violence. He will never punish you. You punish yourself again and again by becoming selfish and by being blind. Now is the time to open your eyes.

Thirdly an angel will say, "Have mercy on yourself." Don't ask for mercy or blessings, love or respect; you have them already. Trust that much, or you will remain a beggar. How has God made you? Not as a beggar, but as a master. So wake up! Wake up!

An angel usually speaks to us through his or her eyes rather than with words. Whether they want to show us love or purity, a feeling of welcome or belonging, they do it through their eyes. When an angel's gaze falls upon you, then you feel that you belong to this family of humanity and are no longer alone. If you look closely into the eyes of an angel, they become like a window. The angel disappears and then you see only God. Have you experienced this?

Just as the eyes of an angel are very powerful, so too are the hands. The hands of an angel give comfort like a little child takes the hand of a parent when the ground is uneven, or they are hurt.

How about the angel in you?

Is it sleeping very deeply at present? Does it wake up from time to time, wanting to do something? If you encounter an obstacle, does it go back to sleep? We have a very pure self inside. Let us cultivate and give attention to it. Let us connect with this pure source of love. You don't need to know much about God; sometimes knowing too much becomes a problem.

All we need to know about God is that He is love, peace, a friend for everyone and never violent. Violence is a human trait; when we fall from elevated consciousness, we become violent towards each other and to nature.

Nature and the earth welcome the angel; they feel the vibrations of an angel, too. Through every step and glimpse, an angel serves. Because they are complete, they don't have to take anything. When we become complete, the angel inside can emerge.

In Brahma Kumaris, we commemorate the founder of the institution (Brahma Baba). He developed the angel inside and so became an example for people to do the same. He had to go into a cocoon to achieve his metamorphosis and maintain a loving link with the Supreme Being. In the beginning, he did not find this easy.

At the time he was teaching, India was bound in the caste system and his teachings, especially about the uplifting of women in society, were revolutionary. He taught us that you can go direct to the Supreme Source; you don't need a guru. He said that human beings are souls and that God is the Supreme Soul. God does not take a physical form, has no religion and needs no worship. It's we who need worship! We act as if the more candles we light, the better He can see us, and the louder we pray, the better He can hear us. It doesn't work like that; it is more subtle.

The motive in your heart draws you closer to the truth. Your country, gender, religion and education do not matter. Only the motive and the purity of your heart.

Brahma Baba had to face many difficult situations while keeping to his principles and acting non-violently. It is not always easy to love our enemies, is it? But the more confidence we have in ourselves, the less the opposition of others will throw us off-course. This is being elevated. Though they may act like enemies, no one is my enemy. We can learn from the people who act like enemies – they become our teachers.

So, whatever you wish for – protection, company, love – you can call on God and you can call on angels. To have a relationship with God means becoming angelic. It requires a great deal of purity, but the connection with God is cleansing. Think of it as a giant vacuum cleaner that reaches every corner of your mind and removes all the dust.

We can be whatever we wish to become because the door of opportunity is open now – today. Don't wait for next year. If we waste time, words or thoughts, we will lack peace of mind and time.

The first step in becoming an angel is silence.

Real silence, not desperate silence, not 'I'm fed up' silence, not rejecting silence but happy, creative silence in which we connect to ourselves and feel connected to God. That kind of silence produces an atmosphere that welcomes and serves others.

Silence is about connecting, feeling full and offering gifts to others with a touch, a glance, a word or a smile. Isn't that easier than all the words we keep saying to fix misunderstandings?

Learn to speak through silence, not through your tongue. This is what the human soul who becomes an angel learns.

MICHAEL'S STORY

PART I

THE ANCIENT CALL

Humanism was not wrong in thinking that truth, beauty, liberty and equality are of infinite value, but in thinking that man can get them for himself without grace.

Simone Weil

The frenetic wind pounded his icy fist against the houses, rattled the narrow streets and impudently smacked people's faces as it galloped across the small town of Pietrasanta.

As the last rays of the winter scurried off under the dark horizon, a young boy found himself wandering, guarding himself against the cruel cold in his thick, blue coat.

The moon, ballooning in the ebony darkness, shone like a pearl in a silver-splattered sky, but Michael did not notice as he rambled under its perfectly round light. He was seventeen years old, and his turquoise-coloured eyes held the quiet sorrow of his loneliness.

Michael's mind wandered back to his parents who had recently died. He thought about his uncle Malfatto, with whom Michael had been sent to live after his parents' death. His uncle did not want him and sent Michael away to find an apprenticeship – anywhere with anyone who would take him. However, no one wanted an apprentice; neither the baker, the gardener, the painter, the jeweller, or the goldsmith. He had tried everywhere.

Some told Michael he was too old, others said that he was too young. Some said he was too thin, others said that his hands were too delicate. Some said he did not look clever enough, others said that he seemed too smart. Michael could see that, for whatever the reason, nobody wanted him or needed him.

Nevertheless, he kept searching every day, though in his heart he did not know what he really wanted. Truth be told, he did not have much of a choice; he had to take whatever was offered. Consequently he lacked enthusiasm and the people he approached noticed.

Over the past few weeks, Michael had lodged in a tiny room in the attic of an inn. Soon he would not be able to afford the rent. Every night he had sat silently in that candle-lit room, pondering what he would do. How long would it take to find an apprenticeship, he asked himself? Why was he stuck in a place where he knew no one? Hardly anyone showed him kindness except the innkeeper who gave him a free meal every evening. Often it was his only meal of the day.

Whenever he sat in the dark loneliness of his room Michael remembered his gentle mother. She had always told him that he was never alone, that God was like a father, or an invisible friend watching over him. But Michael was not so sure he believed in God.

He could not see Him. He needed someone tangible to see and talk with. What's more, seeing the unhappy state of people's hearts, he wondered what God, if He did exist, was doing? Maybe He had become tired of people and found life difficult too? Was that why the world had become like it was?

Tonight, as he walked back towards the inn, Michael found himself in a small street he had not noticed before. "I must have taken a wrong turn," he muttered to himself. He looked around. Yes, this was the right street, so why did everything seem so unfamiliar?

As he looked for the inn, Michael thought he heard faint moans, calls for help. But there did not seem to be anyone around. Walking further, he saw a small stone house in the bright moonlight. Actually it looked more like a hut. He had never seen anything like it in that town. Pietrasanta was not such a big place and he had walked all the streets looking for work.

As he drew closer to the house, the moaning sound grew louder. He reached a broken gate and looked at a garden. It was dreadfully unkempt. Thorny wild rose vines crept everywhere, the weeds were nearly as tall as he was and rats scampered into corners. The door of the house was nearly off its hinges, the window panes were cracked or broken and the roof was full of holes. What a mess, he thought. Who could live here? Someone obviously did because the moans were coming from inside.

Michael stopped at what was left of the broken gate, thinking, "I could get some work here fixing this place."

The moans became louder and he felt compelled to help if he could. But should he? He had learned not to trust anything or anyone too much lately.

Just a few days ago three youths from the town had pretended to be his friends but when they asked if he had any money he understood their real intention. He told them he was looking for an apprenticeship to earn money and they quickly left. So maybe this moaning was a trick played by thieves to get him inside and rob him? Anything could happen these days!

Anyway, Michael did not have so much in his pocket, just a few coins that had to last the whole of the coming month. He put his hand in his tattered pocket. When he felt the coins, tears came to his eyes. He remembered his beloved father, who had given him a bag of coins just before he died. In the depths of his heart Michael believed that people were good, like his parents and the innkeeper, Signor Bianci.

Michael's parents had died along with most of the other inhabitants of Fiesole as a result of a great sickness that had spread through the village. Just before he died, his father had given him the coins and told him to go to his uncle and grandmother, who lived in the country. He cautioned him to keep quiet about the bag of coins.

When he arrived there, sure enough, the first thing his uncle asked was whether his father had given him any money or left a will. As his uncle's greedy eyes flashed, Michael remembered his father's words and said "No".

Uncle Malfatto's bushy eyebrows met, his mouth spread open and downwards, exposing missing teeth and a brown, rotten stump. He turned a bright copper colour and boomed, "Then what good are you to me? That brother of mine was so naïve, he knew nothing about how life works. Of course you have no money! Your father talked nonsense, about understanding others and sharing everything you have. In today's world everyone cheats and is for himself. And see the result? He had no money and now he's off-loading his orphan onto me."

Michael's grandmother egged him on, screeching, "Malfatto, watch that boy. Those eyes and that hair, it's not natural. That boy is strange."

It was not long before Michael's uncle threw him out.

Michael was ready to say the nastiest things to his uncle but he stopped, remembering what his father had taught him about respect. "Michael, speak respectfully to your uncle and grandmother; they are older than you." Michael thought they were so ill-mannered that they did not deserve his respect but he loved his father and so he obeyed.

The moans woke him from his day-dreaming, "Help! Somebody help!"

Michael put the fear of being robbed or beaten out of his mind and opened the gate. He walked up to the battered door and pushed it easily aside.

On the floor he saw a very old woman with a weathered face. Her head was bleeding and she had scratches all over her wrinkled hands. She was struggling to stand up, but this was more than her old bones could manage.

As Michael came in, she looked up and he could see that her face was covered in small scars. Her grey eyes, though almost lifeless, were very kind and her long white hair fell down her bony shoulders and hung around her waist.

Michael went up to the old woman and gently picked her up. She seemed as fragile as thin glass. He sat her on a wobbly wooden chair beside a rickety table and sat beside her. He took out his clean white handkerchief, wiped her face and applied it to the deep cut on her forehead. He kept it there, pressing until the blood stopped flowing.

She reminded him of his grandmother, Nonna Sybila, who constantly complained about everything and made his mother feel tired.

"Be careful of that boy," Nonna Sybila would say. "He has those funny-coloured eyes and that black hair. No one in our family has ever looked like that. It's strange, very strange."

Or, "This pizza is too salty. This pasta does not have enough sauce. The chair is too hard." Michael hoped this old lady was not the same.

"Are you all right?" Michael asked. The house smelled damp and a stale odour hung in the air.

"I have been here a long time, crying out for help, but no one came. Thank you for helping me. Thank you… thank you…."

The old woman sat as best she could and just kept repeating the same words.

To change the conversation, Michael asked her name.

"My name is Aditi," she said quietly.

It was not an Italian name. Michael looked at her closely. She had recovered a little and, as her grey eyes met his, a ray of moonlight caught her face and with it she seemed to gain strength.

"Young man," she started, quietly.

Michael jolted. It was the first time someone had called him "young man". It was always "boy." "Boy do this." or "Boy come here."

"I have a few questions for you," she continued.

At this hour and in her situation Michael hardly thought it appropriate. Besides, he had only come in to help, not to sit an exam.

"You mean like a test?" frowned Michael.

"It's not really a test. Let's call it a game. That will make it more enjoyable."

Michael suddenly had the strange feeling that she had been waiting for him. But how could that be possible? He quickly erased the thought.

The old lady continued, "I have three questions. You must answer each with just one word. Understand? Just one word."

Michael nodded, thinking that maybe the old lady was a little crazy.

So she asked the first question, "What is the purest thing in the world?"

Michael could not think of an answer. He pressed his mind to search for it. "The most pure thing? The purest thing?" he murmured.

He recalled how his parents accepted him and stood by him no matter what anyone said about him. For example, when his teachers told them that he was a hopeless dreamer who did not pay attention and was too slow and hardly spoke, they said to him, "We know that you are much more than what people see. It is just a matter of time; you will show everyone."

Michael blurted out, "The purest thing in the world is loyalty; faithfulness from the ones who truly love you."

"Perfect," replied the old lady, "but remember one-word answers. Next question. Who is your worst enemy? Who is your greatest friend?"

Michael thought this was an easy question and replied, "Yourself."

"Very good," smiled the old lady. Michael noticed how white her teeth were and in what good condition, compared with those of his grandmother and uncle.

"Next question. What pleases God and people most?"

Michael thought for a while. What would he say pleased him most? What did he value most in other people?

"Honesty," he answered.

"Very, very good young man."

Then the old lady looked at him and asked, "What is the one thing that creates all three?"

Without hesitation, Michael replied, "Love."

"You have understood the key." The old lady smiled. "Now let's go further."

Although Michael knew that he must be respectful, he was tired and did not want to continue. He did not remember her name since it was foreign-sounding and difficult to memorise.

"Aditi," she reminded him.

So, she can read thoughts, Michael realised. He must now be careful of his thoughts as well as his answers.

"Aditi, it's been a long day and I am rather tired. Could we continue tomorrow?"

"No, young man, it has to be now. Time is short and every moment counts."

She said this with such conviction that Michael could not say "No". He began to feel that she was giving him an opportunity that he must take. He knew it would not come again, although he still did not understand the nature of the opportunity.

"Yes. Okay. Let's continue," he said.

Suddenly, in the blink of an eye, he saw many objects strewn on the table in front of them. Aditi collected and grouped them together. There was a ruby, a diamond, an emerald and a sapphire.

"Young man, look carefully at each one. Think what it means to you. Then choose one and tell me why you chose it."

Michael was becoming lethargic. He could not concentrate. This always happened to him late at night. All he wanted to do was to go to sleep, but he remembered the old lady's words, "Time is short," and so he gazed on each of the beautiful jewels in turn.

The dark red of the ruby was magnificent. It looked so kingly among the others and its strong red colour pulsed with life. The dark blue of the sapphire reminded him of the freedom of the sky and ocean. The birds and the fish had a freedom he felt he did not have at all. The clear crystal of the diamond was stunning, nothing was hidden there, all was clear and transparent. The brilliant green of the emerald amazed him because it also had a sparkle of blue in it, like a touch of sapphire. As it dazzled him he thought of newness, rebirth and resurrection. It was difficult to choose between the jewels but, finally, Michael chose the emerald.

"I see," said the old lady, "that explains it."

"Explains what?" asked Michael.

As he waited for her to explain the significance of his choice she moved on to something else. Suddenly a new set of objects appeared on the table. All the others, except the emerald , which Michael held in his hand, had gone.

Now in front of him were a golden sword, a silver compass, a small wooden clock in the shape of a wheel and a book with a bright scarlet cover.

"Choose the one you like best," the woman commanded. "Choose. Quickly, quickly!"

"What's the hurry?" he thought. He was sure she was not saying this because it was late and she needed to sleep. But he did not say anything. Somehow he knew not to question her with his many "whys?" even though he had a lot. Why was he here? Why was he playing this ridiculous game at this hour when he should be sleeping? Why was she dressed in white? Why was she giving him these tests?

He looked at the objects. The sword promised victory and its golden beauty beckoned him. The compass was essential for finding the right direction and he sure needed some at this stage of his life. From the wooden clock he saw the hands of time calling him to do something, to be something. Finally he picked up the scarlet book. Opening it he saw that all the pages were blank. Surely this was the least useful of the four?

"Quickly young man. Before midnight. Before midnight," Aditi insisted.

Michael disliked her pushiness and the alarm about midnight. It reminded him of Cinderella. Would she turn into the fairy godmother, the house into a pumpkin and he into a rat? He wanted to tell her she was distracting him but, instead of saying anything, he returned his attention to the objects.

He kept gazing but still could not choose. Just as he was about to pick up the beautiful golden sword, the emerald he was holding sent out a green-blue ray that made the scarlet book glow in a crown of vermillion. His hand went to the book even though his mind was on the sword.

Again, everything disappeared except the scarlet book. Why had he chosen that? Why had he been compelled to choose this book with its totally blank pages?

"Quick, quick," the old woman appealed. "Let us continue before midnight comes."

Another test! Michael thought. He was getting irritated. How long were these so-called games to continue? He started to protest when he heard the reassuring words, "This is the final game."

In front of him, Michael saw four flowers: a huge yellow sunflower, triumphant and glorious; a violet, its lovely mauve face speaking of silence and humility; an immaculate white rose which looked as if a hundred round snowflakes had been threaded onto its green stem; and finally a crimson iris. This looked as if two or three butterflies were sitting together with their long, curved wings pointing upwards and downwards. So beautiful. Michael remembered that Iris was the goddess of the rainbow.

Again he was perplexed but, suddenly, as the moon spread her ivory mantle over the table, the rose shone with a translucent whiteness beyond any whiteness he had ever seen. He gently picked it up. It was immaculate and in its radiance was even more beautiful than the emerald.

"Aha, I knew it," spoke Aditi. "I have been calling for years and only tonight was I heard."

Michael was surprised, "Were you on the ground for years?" He could not really believe it.

"Oh my child…"

"There's a change", thought Michael; "until recently I was 'young man'".

"Oh my child," she continued, "for more years than I can remember I have been lying here bleeding, neglected, misused."

Michael was shocked, "By whom?"

"I am afraid to say by your race, Michael – Adam's progeny."

Michael felt this was unjust. He was not to blame for what had happened to her.

"The Great Lord of Life promised that on this day, in this year, before the clock strikes midnight, a worthy one from Adam's race would appear to restore the rightful order – or it would be too late."

Michael said, "What has that got to do with me?"

"My child, you are that worthy one from the direct root of Adam, your father."

"No!" exclaimed Michael. "My father's name was Luca and he was born, lived and died in Fiesole. Enough of this! I need to go because I have to look for work tomorrow."

"In spite of your cleverness, you have not understood, have you?"

Aditi smiled. She smiled like his mother used to smile when he got upset, a smile that comforted him. But Michael was puzzled.

"What am I supposed to understand? Here I am walking home, minding my own business. This strange house appears. I hear your moans. I come in and, before you know it, I am presented with these tests or 'games' as you call them, which I have to answer before midnight. Now, if you were me, would you think all this is normal?"

Aditi kept smiling. "Now I will tell you the significance of your choices and then you will understand. And we will finish before midnight."

She is so obsessed with midnight, Michael thought. Is she really a fairy godmother? Right now I could use one!

"The emerald is a deep sea green but has a sky-blue vein," Aditi explained. "This colour is so exceptionally rare that it makes it more valuable than any other stone, even a diamond. It means rebirth; it is the colour of paradise and symbolises peace, healing, faith and hope for something better in the world. And, son of Osiris, you will be reborn and conquer all illusions. This will herald the springtime of a new world."

Michael liked the idea of spring and something new. She was right, this green-blue emerald was one of the most beautiful things he had ever seen. But what was this about Osiris? She was mixing up the name of his father again. First Adam, now Osiris. Should he tell her again that his father's name was Luca?

She continued, "And the bright scarlet book…"

Yes, thought Michael, the one with the blank pages. That wasn't completely my choice.

"Did you notice the colour, child?"

Yes he had. It was a bright blood red and it glowed at him, or so he imagined.

"Scarlet is the symbol of sacrifice."

"Does that mean I have to die, or something?" asked Michael in alarm.

"Yes, Michael, you have to die."

"But I don't want to yet. You told me this was all a game. Dying doesn't sound like much of a game to me!"

"No, Michael. Tonight you will learn what it means to die."

"But when you die you're dead! That's it!"

Aditi explained patiently, "To die means to let go of your old self, the self that creates fear, hopelessness, anger and resentment. I am sure you want to get rid of these things. However, for this to truly happen you have to 'die' or 'let go' every day."

"How?" asked Michael, confused.

"Take the scarlet book. Every day you must write on a page. In the morning write, 'What is my aim or my change today?' And in the evening, write, 'What did I accomplish today?' or 'What could have been better?'"

"Is that all?" asked Michael, relieved.

"Yes, that is all. But that is everything. You have to check to see how you pass your daily tests to gauge where you are. It's easy, but it's also difficult, because it can be easily forgotten."

Michael had thought he had to do something really difficult, something far more strenuous or harder, like giving up pizza or gelato.

"And now the flowers", she said. The pearl-coloured rose sat in a small glass vase. Michael did not know how it got there but there it was - its white face glimmering in the moonlight.

"This rose, Michael, symbolises your heart. It is pure. It is honest. It is trusted by God and, although you have endured many bitter things in your life, your innocence has remained."

Michael had often heard the opposite from different people, so he was rather surprised to hear Aditi's words. But, as she was speaking, he felt something stirring inside. She was helping him to recognise things that he somehow knew or had forgotten. The emerald in his palm shone and the scarlet book glowed.

She continued, "It is midnight and the search has been completed. The Great Lord will be pleased."

"Great Lord?" asked Michael. It was the first he had heard of him. "Who is the Great Lord?"

"The One who never dies, the One who is constant Light, the One who is Love, the One…"

Michael interrupted, "Do you mean God?"

"Yes," she said. At that point he heard the church clock begin to strike 12. With each stroke, the light of the moon shone intensely on Aditi and Michael could not believe what he saw.

At each stroke of the clock, the old Aditi was becoming younger. Her hair, strand by strand, gradually turned black. Her eyes started to shine and turned the colour of the emerald, sometimes dark blue, sometimes deep green. Her skin became a soft brown and her dress became new and dazzling blue-green, the same colour as her eyes.

Now she spoke, "I am Lady Aditi. The cycle of time has returned to its beginning and I am free again."

She turned to Michael, "All that had to finish by midnight or, instead of becoming younger, I would have aged and died. Now Michael, it is your turn to transform."

Michael marvelled at her youth and beauty, "But I am already young. I do not need to transform, Lady Aditi."

"No, Michael, your transformation is not like mine. It is different."

With her words, Michael felt an ancient call inside, a destiny calling him to remember and to become his true self. Although he felt something was to change and that he had to do it, he did not know what it was.

Lady Aditi continued, "Michael, from this moment you are an apprentice of the Great Lord. He will help you remember what you have forgotten and what you must become again. He will bring you into the Light of Truth."

"An apprentice to become what?" Michael asked.

"An angel," Lady Aditi replied.

"A what?" he gulped.

He had seen angels in the churches in Fiesole, Pietrasanta and many other places across Italy. They were all shapes, sizes and colours and were doing different things. In spite of the variety they had one thing in common, they all had wings. He did not think he could grow wings! Not just yet anyway.

He decided to be serious with himself. The way Lady Aditi spoke moved Michael's soul to its depth. Instead of doubting, he asked, "How?"

She quickly replied, "It takes a great deal of learning and letting go of your old, small self. You will learn to serve as a generous instrument of Divine Love to all the souls of Earth, God's children, who are your brothers and sisters. However, you need to study, Michael, and you have to start very, very soon."

"Where?" he asked.

"Here," she answered.

Michael was a little disturbed. Here in this rundown house? Surely God could find a better workplace? He looked around: the walls needed painting, the windows and doors needed fixing and there was probably no water. What a classroom!

"What time do I start?" he enquired.

"Four o'clock tomorrow morning."

"What!" he thought he had misheard. "You mean four o'clock tomorrow afternoon?"

Lady Aditi, in her dazzling turquoise beauty, looked at him, "No, four o'clock in the morning, just before the dawn, the freshest and purest time of the day. Your first thoughts will go to the Great Lord and you will hear Him very clearly at that hour. It is called the hour of ambrosia, the immortal time. You will drink the sacred *soma* of the immortals."

"But I might fall asleep at such an early hour. I may not even wake up!" he argued. He had to think of other excuses. "It's cold and dark and dangerous if I have to walk here every morning. There may be robbers."

"Do not worry, Michael. I will give you Sekhmet. She will walk with you every morning."

A large ginger-red cat appeared and sat next to Michael, waiting for directions.

"A cat to protect me?" He had assumed Sekhmet was a dog.

"What can a cat do?"

As he looked into the cat's eyes, they seemed as red as her coat, as if telling him to go beyond what he could see and find out who she really was. But all that Michael could see was a cat.

"So, Michael, go back to the inn. Be here tomorrow at four o'clock and the Great Lord will be here to give you your first lesson. Take the emerald and book with you. Keep the stone in your pocket and use it to feel people and situations. It is like your third eye. When you remember it, your ability to perceive will expand. Then no one and nothing can deceive you."

As Michael looked at the emerald it glowed the same colour as Lady Aditi's eyes. For a moment he felt the emerald reflecting the colour of his own eyes – it really was his third eye!

"Take the book with you. You can start writing from tomorrow."

He looked at her, saw she wasn't joking and put the scarlet book in his pocket next to the emerald.

"The white rose will remain here. If you have learned your lesson well it will shed a petal. When every petal has been shed you will be ready. Then you will no longer be an apprentice, but an angel, ready to serve. However, the rose may not shed a petal for weeks; it all depends on how you progress."

Michael accepted everything Lady Aditi said. Though he did not understand it all, he knew it was right. In time things would become clear.

He said goodnight to Lady Aditi, made sure the emerald and book were in his pocket, and left the small stone house via the broken gate. He walked out onto the street in the bright moonlight with Sekhmet following a few metres behind. He was somewhat amused with his cat "watchdog".

As Michael neared the inn, he wanted to see the emerald in the moonlight. He took it out of his pocket. It shone such a bright green and sometimes glittered blue; Michael felt he had one of the most precious things in the world. As he held it, he felt the hidden pulse of nature beating.

He suddenly heard voices behind him.

"Well, the boy has come into an inheritance, we see. Was it from your father? Tell us the truth boy; you stole it didn't you?" And the voices laughed.

The voices seemed familiar. As Michael turned around he recognised them as the three youths who had asked for his money a week or so before. They approached, smirking.

"Give us your pretty stone, boy!"

Michael defiantly put the stone in his pocket and was about to run when they jumped on him and pulled him to the ground.

"Don't want to share your inheritance with your friends?" laughed one, grabbing at Michael's pocket. "Selfish aren't you, wanting to keep things for yourself?"

"Stop struggling so much," he shouted and was about to land Michael a punch while the others held down his arms and legs. Suddenly they heard an enormous roar, looked up and froze in horror as they saw a huge lioness with sharp teeth and claws approach, ready to pounce on them. Screaming in fear, they let go of Michael and ran off.

Michael had also seen the lioness ready to jump. Closing his eyes, he was sure this was his end. He lay thinking it would have been better to die at the hands of the thieves rather than in the huge mouth of a wild beast. He kept his eyes closed as he felt a hot breath on his face. Then suddenly he felt a very sticky lick.

He opened his eyes to see Sekhmet looking down at him. Grasping the emerald he was able, for a split second, to see Sekhmet's true nature. She was a protector, as Lady Aditi had promised.

Michael got up and picked up the cat. With his face to the buffeting icy wind, he walked home quickly. Arriving at the inn, he opened the door and quietly went to his room.

Signor and Signora Bianci were very kind to him. Michael

felt blessed to stay in their inn. The attic room they had given him was small with a table, a chair and tiny wardrobe. He did not need a big one because he had only two pairs of trousers, two pairs of socks, one blue winter coat and two shirts.

He was not sure if they allowed cats in the inn but he put Sekmet on a small mat near his bed. Then he put the book and the emerald on the table.

The skylight made him especially love this room. He looked up at the stars. When sad he looked at them glittering in the black, silk sky and his loneliness would disappear. He considered the stars to be his special, silver friends. They shone soft light onto his face and into his heart.

Anyway, now there was not much time for sleep if he was to be up at a quarter to four and be on time for his first lesson with Lady Aditi and the Great Lord.

Michael did not sleep very much that night.

Was there really such a Lady Aditi, or he had dreamed it? Why so early in the morning? Something must be wrong.

"School", she had said. But no normal school opens at four in the morning, he thought to himself.

This is not a normal school, he remembered her saying. Did she tell him this or did he dream it? Lady Aditi was certainly not a normal person, changing age and dress as she did.

Michael felt uncertain and doubts started to eat at him.

What should he do? Go? Or try to sleep and just pretend it did not happen?

As he looked in the corner of the room where Sekmet lay, he saw that she was sitting up as if waiting for him to get going. Still Michael was not sure.

As he looked up at the stars, he suddenly saw what looked like an oval light, much bigger than the other stars. The Great Star was sending rays of light into his mind and he heard a voice encouraging him. "Michael rise. Go now. Take this opportunity".

The voice, or rather the thought from the oval light, inspired and soothed him. He quickly dressed and silently left the inn with Sekmet by his side.

He hurried along the small street to Lady Aditi's school. Something, like a magnet, was pulling him in the right direction and he did not have to think how to find his way there. Sekmet walked slightly in front of him showing him the way.

When he arrived at the door of the school, it looked different. Things had been fixed. There were no broken doors or windows and tall, beautiful roses and lilies of different colours were growing in the garden, which looked much bigger. Was he at the right place? Sekmet reassured him in the way that only cats can.

As he approached the door, it opened by itself to welcome

him and he entered a room where Lady Aditi was waiting. The room of the previous night had completely changed - a honey-coloured carpet, filled the entire room with some ivory-coloured cushions for sitting.

As he sat in the presence of Lady Aditi, an orb of bright light appeared in front of him and a voice from the light spoke to him. It was the Great Lord of Life.

"Welcome Michael, you are the first apprentice at the school. Let me introduce Myself.

I am pure consciousness
Living Light
You can only meet Me when I reveal Myself to you
I show the Way

With My coming begins the Age of Confluence
I guide and inspire souls to:
Remember
Transform and
Return to their original spiritual self
Their original freedom

I am
The Being without a body
The Point of Light
The Eternal Energy who
Reveals the original truth
Dissolves illusion and
Sustains the genuine

I am One
You are one of many
I am eternally beyond change
I am never bound in the circle of time like you

I am the Eternal Reference Point
For every beginning and every end

I am the Zero
The Numberless Being
You are all numbers
Constant expression through time, matter and sound is your destiny

I am the Living Seed
The Immortal Blueprint
For renaissance and newness
Know Me and you will know yourself
Understand Me and you will understand yourself.
Although I am not you, I am like you

I am not found in everything
But everything depends on Me
For regeneration and
Return to the original pure state

I am the One who is
Knowledgeful
Blissful
Uncreated

I am the Universal Father and
Mother of all humanity

Through union with Me
You will regain your self-respect and lost divinity.
Connect your mind with My Mind
From a pure state of mind
Love and wisdom are born and shared."

Michael sat in awe. His eyes shone and tears of love streamed down his cheeks as he listened to the words of the Great Lord. He felt so peaceful and happy inside. All his troubles and doubts had melted away and for the first time in many months he felt safe, secure and at home.

His apprenticeship had begun!

MICHAEL'S JOURNAL

THE MINDSET AND PRACTICES OF AN ANGEL

Very little is needed to make a happy life; it is all within yourself, in your way of thinking.
Marcus Aurelius

I am keeping a journal in this sparkling scarlet book. Every day, as Lady Aditi suggested, I will write down my thoughts, feelings, experiences and reflections, as well as notes from Lady Aditi's classes, the words of the Great Lord and the strange voice I hear sometimes in my head. In this way I hope to capture all that I need to do and be in order to pass this apprenticeship and become an angel.

UNDERSTANDING GOD

We met the Great Lord today. He is so sweet and humble. I love Him so much.

During the few weeks I have been at the school we've met with Him many times. I have learned so much from Him and Lady Aditi.

I've noticed that He tends to let Lady Aditi do most of the teaching because she has studied with Him for many years and knows Him so well.

I experience His invisible presence. He is always with me, especially early in the morning when I sit with Him in silence and feel His gentle embrace.

He has melted my heart.

I now realise that my previous ideas of God were so wrong.

He's not an old man in the sky waiting to punish me and send me to hell forever.

He is not a God of fear or force.

He only wants what is best for me.

He is an Ocean of Love

An Ocean of Peace and

An Ocean of Knowledge

I understand His role more clearly.

He has come to remind us of our greatness and to restore us back to our original pure spiritual self.

It is only at this time that we have the opportunity to experience Him directly.

He guides and inspires me to make my own decisions and choices.

So much has been said and done in God's name and many people don't believe in Him and some even hate Him! But I can see now that the real problem is not God's existence, but the lack of love between all of us.

Pause for Reflection

What is your understanding of God?
What part does God play in your life?
What more do you want to understand about God?

HUMANS AND ANGELS

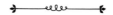

Today the Great Lord spoke to us about angels. He said that becoming an angel is a very special thing. It is our destiny to be His special companions and help the world in this time of need. He will reveal all the secrets of perfection and take us on a journey to become angels. And then He explained the difference between human beings and angels.

- Humans ask, angels trust
- Humans analyse, angels know
- Humans wait, angels create
- Humans judge, angels discern
- Humans separate, angels embrace
- Humans correct, angels inspire
- Humans learn, angels remember
- Humans process, angels understand
- Humans measure, angels donate
- Humans justify, angels reconcile
- Humans defend, angels accept
- Humans diagnose, angels heal
- Humans criticise, angels empathise

- Humans love, angels cherish
- Humans think, angels feel
- Humans speculate, angels realise
- Humans hear, angels listen
- Humans speak, angels are silent

Knowing the difference between human beings and angels enables me to focus my attention and aim in the right direction.

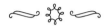

Pause for Reflection

Which of these statements resonate with you?
How do they uplift and inspire you?
Would you like to become more angelic and less human?
In what ways?

Meditation (1)

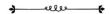

I have learned that God is a point of spiritual light – a Being of consciousness the same as ourselves! The only difference is that the Supreme Soul does not enter a body and take re-birth and is thus able to remain beyond the drama of this physical world and be an unlimited source of spiritual energy that we can tap into.

When we realise who we really are, we are able to understand the nature of God.

Today we did the following meditation:

Close your mind, shut your ears, and retreat from the world. Just concentrate. Then silently say to yourself the following words:

I relax my body
I relax my mind

Gently, very gently, I concentrate on the centre of my forehead
I visualise there a point of light

I begin the journey into deep silence to meet my original self
I ask "Who am I?"
In the silence, I remember that I am a spiritual being

I am a soul
My original nature is peace and harmony
I am free from anything wasteful
I am free from the past
I concentrate on the essential part of me
The soul
A point of living energy

I am peace
Pure, deep peace
I am light, peace, harmony, silence

In this awareness I connect with the Supreme Source of love
I remember this original friendship
I experience the presence of the Eternal One
His light
His love
His silence
Love, light, silence
This will heal me

FLYING

Today Lady Aditi spoke to us of flying.

Many of us begin the apprenticeship of spirituality motivated by an urge simply to become peaceful. Others feel a calling to become a spiritual teacher and venture no further. Some will stop when they achieve sainthood or become a hero, but others want more than this. Lady Aditi believes that anyone can become an angel, if they really want to.

Angels are nearly always depicted with wings. The wings are not literal but symbolic. Angels are subtle beings of light. Through the power of their mind they have the ability to travel through time and space. As instruments or messengers of God, they give support as and when required.

So one of the characteristics of an angel is their ability to fly, to serve others whenever and wherever necessary.

At this moment, time signals to us that we can learn to fly.

What creates our capacity for flight?

✣ Experience of the soul-self

✣ Freedom from subservience

✣ A constant receiving of the Divine current

Angels remove sorrow; they never get entangled in it.

We cannot serve anyone or anything we are attached or stuck to. 'Sticking' in this way is a selfish need that we try to disguise by using the word 'mercy'. Real mercy never sticks.

An angel is taught by God to care, support and protect others, whilst simultaneously developing personal responsibility and an autonomous state of mind.

We have the capacity to be so generous that God can use our heart to guide many to the Source of Love.

The height of our flight depends on the extent to which we are willing to let go of our false self... especially those spots of pettiness and selfishness that cover us at the moment. These can easily be removed.

This time is blessed. We can reach as high as a midday sun and then our rays will spread very, very far. However, if we stay on the horizon of self-absorption, our light will only reach a few people.

What will move us above any complacency? Compassion.

Altitude depends so much on having a loving attitude, not on knowledge. We must:

- ❇ Practice flying in our mind

- ❇ Go beyond all limits

- ❇ Break the barrier and

- ❇ Conquer gravity

Because so many need light now. So many...

When we fly beyond, we enter Eternity and bring its gift of light into time, nature and our human family.

The height of our flight depends on the depth of our spirituality.

We must stabilise our mind with full will and concentration on the authentic self, the soul. Unless this is done, we may occasionally jump up but, like a frog, we will land in the same position. This will result in a few croaks of achievement but nothing really benevolent.

Progress is not just about moving outward, savouring a few experiences and discovering a few new things. These intellectual or emotional thrills are quite deceptive. We must always remain conscious of our spiritual origins – keep them constantly in our awareness. We need to go beyond the intellect and emotions to touch the conscious core of our soul – otherwise everything we call 'progress' is only an illusion.

Illusion acts like a slow poison that saps our strength simply because it is not true. Faith in falsehood leads to slow degradation and eventually to hell. We need to be attentive so that in every flight we always remain connected to our spiritual base. The higher we fly, the deeper we must stabilise ourselves.

Meditation (2)

Become still, peaceful and serene. Then silently say to yourself the following words:

Om Shanti (I am a peaceful soul)

With the knowledge of my original peaceful self, I step inside and connect via my thoughts to that which is originally pure in the self.

In this connective silence there are no leakages and, therefore, no imbalances.

I am at peace with myself.

This is the essential first step to experiencing the ambrosia of spiritual bliss.

Bliss is contentment, love and serenity all combined and experienced in the relationship with God.

Manmanabhav

God says to the soul, "Be mine with your mind."
This is the exercise for divine experience.

Through this exercise the human soul receives the divine current, the miraculous flow of energy, the ambrosia.

Manmanabhav is the purest and most liberating thought a human soul can create.

Through this thought the magic current is received and I am gradually moulded into an angelic being.

By repeating this thought I am taught to:
Appear and disappear
Be still and fly
Speak and be silent
Be generous and be economical
See and not see
Hear and not hear
Embrace and let go
Remember and forget -
All according to Divine guidance
And humanity's need

TIPS FOR SAFE FLYING

This flying business is not as easy as I thought. I have been more like a frog than an eagle so I went to see Lady Aditi and she offered the following advice:

- ❋ I must not just move away, but fly away from useless things. In other words, I must not entertain bad habits or make excuses.
- ❋ If I do not have any threads of attachment, others cannot pull me.
- ❋ Passion is narcissism! (I need to think more about this one.)
- ❋ I will not waste time with people who create cages as they will definitely invite me in!
- ❋ I must go beyond myself in order to find myself. (What does this mean?)
- ❋ It is not necessary to talk, just to change (easier said than done as I love talking!)
- ❋ The behaviour of someone indicates what they have learned.

- ❄ If I expect others to change, it is because I am too weak to change myself.
- ❄ When I change, I find the solution.
- ❄ By using or thinking the words "mine" and "my", I create the wrong sense of responsibility and then try to play saviour or do-gooder.
- ❄ Only that which is clean can work. (I need to clean up my mind and my heart.)

I love these teachings! They will help me soar like an eagle over the challenges of living in this world.

Pause for Reflection

Imagine what it would be like to be an angel and use the power of your mind to serve humanity. Where would you fly and whom would you serve?

If you could appear in people's dreams in their hour of need what would be your message?

Which of the tips for flying interest you? Why?

DOUBT

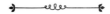

The Great Lord has on many occasions warned us about the dangers of doubt. He says it is like a cancer. It can spread quickly and easily through the mind and completely destroy the faith we have in ourselves and in our ability to grow spiritually and become the angel we are meant to be. The old ego-based self resists the new ways of thinking and being and does its best to crush them.

Today I had my first attack of doubt. It was awful. Until now I thought I was doing well. I have been so happy, enthusiastic and excited about my future, full of faith that I am on the right track. But now I am not so sure.

This is what I remember of the conversation.

"Fly? *You* fly? What an absurd aim. You are just a human. You can crawl, walk, stroll, run, jump, ride, swim, even gallop, but you certainly cannot fly!

At the moment your mind is full of fantasy, your intellect is confused, your heart has always been full of the past, of wounds, of people. To have only God in there has never been your practice; believe me, it's not for you. This angelic business is a phantom of your ego."

I was so shocked that I could think like this. It kept going.

"Look in the mirror, yes, take a good look. The mirror reveals all. There you are: a body, a face and so many masks – so many it's not worth trying to count them all! You are your role, you are your body and, especially, you are your social identity. The basis of true happiness is how others see and value you. You have always known that.

Don't play games with yourself. Real humility is to doubt yourself. It is not safe to be so confident. You cannot be something you are not. It is wonderfully imaginative to think of being light and even flying, but it is totally unrealistic."

I listened to the heavy, clever voice pushing me to deny everything I have been experiencing.

"But the Great Lord told me I can be whatever I want to be. He will co-operate, the world is in such great need of Light."

"Oh I see, so you want to play Saviour? Beware, saviours are always made into scapegoats by a selfish mob. This 'saviour' idea is a trap for you.

God does not speak. He told you nothing. It's just a voice inside your head. Be careful. Imagination plays havoc when there is emptiness inside and the need to be a somebody.

Why are you so afraid to be a nobody? In reality everybody is a nobody but no one has the guts to face it. They invent a talking God, an elitist task, a special messenger.

So take it easy. Look in the mirror. Do you see any halo?

You are not light. You are matter.

You are not a soul. You are a body.

You are not eternal. You are just a wisp of breath in time and space, here today and gone tomorrow."

The harsh voice persisted with its clever opinions. It succeeded in rankling me. I was deeply shaken, doubts did arise but I knew that the call to this apprenticeship was not simply my imagination.

I don't like this voice.

Pause for Reflection

How does the voice in your head affect you and hold you back from achieving spiritual goals?

What can you do to overcome it?

THE APPRENTICE'S OATH

Today we made an oath. Lady Aditi told us that making a pledge to follow certain practices regularly and consistently every day is vital for the apprentice angel.

I made the pledge to the Great Lord with great sincerity after spending a lot of time reflecting on whether this was the right path for me. Deep in my heart I know it is. It will require great faith, courage and determination to make it a reality.

Afterwards I felt so good, so sure that I had made the right decision. My face glowed with happiness.

Here is the oath.

I will begin every day by expressing gratitude for this apprenticeship with God

This first thought of my day gives me direction and the courage to meet challenges and to regard everything as an opportunity.

I understand that everything and everyone is my teacher

No matter how difficult, how unexpected, how unwanted the experience, that comes into my life, I ask God "What can I learn from this?" and "What transformation must come about?"

Every two hours I will put a brake on my mind and my tongue

I step inside myself for a minute and become quiet; I stop, relax and observe. Once my understanding is clearer, I can re-enter the flow of daily activities with new-found direction.

As soon as I notice myself complaining and blaming I will stop

These two habits destroy my inner strength because they show that I am still expecting solutions and changes to come from others. Instead, I have to change the way I think, feel, see and act – and especially what and how I choose.

Every day I will give thanks to God, to life and to the universe

Because
I exist
I can learn
I can transform
I can share love

Successfully putting these principles into practice requires humility, an attitude of gratitude, self-discipline and an understanding and acceptance that there is benefit in everything that is happening in my life.

What a wonderful way to live!!

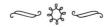

Pause for Reflection

What spiritual principles and practices do you follow in your daily life?

Are there any additions you would like to make having read the above?

THE QUALITIES AND
ROLE OF AN ANGEL

—◦—

*An angel is someone with principles, who moves by
the spirit, not the letter of the law. Angels see the
motive not the move; they see the heart not the words.*

Dadi Janki

For the past few weeks we have been studying in depth the
qualities and awareness required of an angel. It has been very
interesting and it would have been quite daunting without
the gentle support and encouragement of Lady Aditi. We
have also been made to sit for early morning meditation
and I can feel how the subtle injection of power I have been
receiving from the Great Lord at that time has really helped.

This is what I have understood so far.

Pause for Reflection

What are your own thoughts and feelings about angels?
Do you believe in angels?
Have you, or anyone you know, ever had an angelic experience?
If so, describe what happened.

AN ANGEL IS AN INSTRUMENT

An angel is an instrument of God in the same way that a flute is an instrument played by a musician or a scalpel is an instrument used by a surgeon.

This awareness allows us to become egoless and co-operate more effectively with the divine plan.

When I am empty I say
"I do, I have done, I will do."

When I am connected to God
I feel everything is being done
I just happen to be here

A vessel of God's Light
An instrument of His Love
A messenger of His Peace

Angels do this naturally and easily
While serving they have the constant feeling that
"All is done."

AN ANGEL IS HONEST

It is said that the Lord is pleased with an honest heart.

Honesty makes us progress
It motivates us to achieve our full potential

We accumulate inner strength
This leads to generosity

Honesty gives us courage
Then we need never fear anyone or anything

Honesty makes us clear and wise… transparent
An angel must be transparent

Every heartbeat should be seen.

AN ANGEL IS CONTENT

Angels always feel content.

Discontent is a signal that we have wandered off course.
Contentment is the foundation of spiritual power.
It comes when we look inside and appreciate the wonder
of our being: its eternal nature, value and relationship with
God and humanity.

In the NOW of every moment
I am glad to be me
I am grateful for my existence
Such contentment progresses into happiness.

*Every day, it is good to use the thermometer of contentment to
check our spiritual health.*

Pause for Reflection

How content are you – in this moment? In general?
How could you be more content?

ANGELS ARE SENSIBLE

Understanding the basic peaceful nature of the soul enables the angel within to respond in a mature and practical way to the challenges that arise in relationships.

Being sensible means never arguing.

We understand that life is all about conquering the self, not others!

Manipulative and clever language can never prove the truth.

In fact, quite the opposite.

What we are speaks for itself.

When we are sensible no gravity of any kind can pull us down.

We become light.

Being light, we do not battle with anyone.

ANGELS HAVE SELF-RESPECT

Self-respect allows us to be true to ourselves, no matter what.

It gives us the courage and confidence to follow the path to becoming an angel.

When we have self-respect we do not manipulate others, nor do we allow others to manipulate or control us. If someone does manipulate or control us it is because we have given them permission, either out of fear, or because of attachment.

For me self-respect is the most important part of this study.

I realise that without self-respect I can never become an angel.

Pause for Reflection

How much do I respect myself?
If I had greater self-respect what difference would
it make in my life?
How can I increase my self-respect?

ANGELS HAVE PURE VISION

Angels see the specialties of each person, not their weaknesses or what we see as a weakness.

Angels see but do not see, they hear but do not hear.

Whatever comes to us, we must go beyond and do not get stuck in it. When we cannot move, we are unable to help others move.

It is an addiction to blame and justify.

It is arrogance to think we are so clever that we can correct another. Whatever others do is their responsibility.

We are responsible for our attitudes and for developing benevolence, regardless of the behaviour of others.

We have to stop seeing defects and wanting to justify that we are right.

Pause for Reflection

What would your life be like if you were able to have such pure vision of yourself and others?

Think of someone you complain about. How could you change your vision of that person? What difference would it make to the relationship?

THOUGHTS

Today we learned about thoughts. They are the building blocks of consciousness.

We become kinder when we keep our thinking beyond the pettiness that constantly evolves from "I" and "my".

Thoughts filled with kindness and silence are called 'elevated.' They glow with generosity and are all-embracing and inclusive.

We must never allow such triviality in our thinking that we develop mean feelings, or become trapped in the black hole of the small self.

If we keep our thoughts linked to eternity we see life through the Heart of God.

Blindness is cured.

Our eyes receive an unlimited perspective - they become windows of pure thought, emanating uplifting energy for whoever approaches.

Seeing things as they are eternally, we feel the value of all things.

No longer deceived by appearance or quick judgments, we remain conscious of the goodness of others.

HOW TO TRANSFORM
WASTEFUL THOUGHTS

LINK
Do not think
Fewer thoughts means fewer words and more silence
Thoughts cause interference

In the state of concentrated quietness…
In the link with God…
I do not think…
I am

When I link, thoughts no longer trample my mind
In that clean space I become present
Divine radiance fills my being

My existence becomes
An offering
A sharing
An inspiration
A method and
A hope to those around me

It happens naturally without any calculation on my part

When I am so clear
So transparent
So full
People will never doubt that they have met an angel

LISTEN
Tune in
Feel and understand the need
Serve the need
Never exploit it through arrogance or greed
Or get entangled in it through misguided mercy

LEARN
All that happens occurs to bring about change in
The mind
The heart
Our awareness and
The world

LOVE
The more I am, the less I cling
The more I cling, the less I am
Clinging people have forgotten to respect
Their hearts have atrophied

Respect is the foundation of all genuine feelings.

CHECK

I need to be introspective very often and check myself very thoroughly in order to release blind spots, habits, routines and anything that inhibits my progress.

Self-examination refines
It transforms me into light
So that there is
No burden
No shadow
No guilt
No disheartenment
Nothing artificial remains inside me
Just great movements of ascent

CONNECT

When I have a problem, no matter how frightening
When I suffer from weakness, no matter how negative
When a shock hits me, no matter how wrenching
I do not connect with it or get dragged into its whirlwind

With a determined thought
I connect with the original self
Find my peace and stability
Remember God
Feel all His support and strength

When I connect with God
He takes me into Eternity
He offers me the healing gift of *perspective,* one of the most

precious insights on the journey towards wholeness and completeness.

Perspective gives me
Breadth and balance
Clarity to see solutions
Courage to accept certain happenings
Peace to overcome fear
The capacity to know that all this will pass
It enables me to remain stable and free from desperation

Free from wasteful or negative thoughts, words or habits
I am ready to serve again

When I go beyond thinking and speaking
There is only silence and action
True action speaks for itself

This refining of the mind works on our nature and gradually creates spiritual light.

When I learn to recognise unnecessary or negative thoughts, words and the habit of experiencing upheaval over anything, or anyone, then I can change it. This only takes a second.

Remember:
LINK, LISTEN, LEARN, LOVE, CHECK, CONNECT

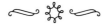

Pause for Reflection

Go inside and notice the thoughts on the screen
of your mind now.

Do these thoughts make you feel happy or sad?
Positive, or negative?

Do they drain or increase your energy?

What effect are they having on your body?
Do you feel tense, relaxed or tired?

If you were to express these thoughts and feelings now,
what impact would they have on yourself and others?

Would they cause happiness or sorrow?
Would they uplift, depress or stress?

Check, are there any thoughts that need to be transformed?

THE THIRD EYE

Thought is subtle and requires daily attention in order for it to be harnessed and used effectively. Thought control requires moment-by-moment *attention* because every day is new and different. So adjustments are required. I need to watch my thoughts in the same way I watch clouds passing by.

It is the most difficult thing to do…to control and hold thought and take it where I want it to go. Often thoughts seem to control me and carry me to places and events I would prefer not to go.

Today Lady Aditi gave us a gift. She came to class with a small jar of yellow paste in her hand. As we sat silently she dipped her finger into the jar and put a golden mark in the centre of each one's forehead.

She said the third eye is the gift of stability.

I can only activate it through concentrated thought.

It is the eye needed to see the hidden, the invisible and the subtle.

It is the eye through which I can feel the Truth of all things.

When activated I can see, that is intuit, the reality of something.

This state of *awareness* is called *soul consciousness*. Because I remain in the awareness of the invisible, I am not deceived by the visible, the external. I can see behind someone's words and actions.

To keep this eye open I must continue to awaken before the dawn every morning and communicate with the Great Lord who will send me the current to keep it open.

The current enables me to see and feel the invisible and the future.

DOUBT AGAIN

I try to connect every morning but sometimes I get it and sometimes I don't.

Lady Aditi has warned us that the spiritual journey has its ups and downs. There will be times when we feel disconnected from the truth and disappointed in our progress. We know where we are going and how we are meant to be but the gap between the present and the future state of the soul can seem so great that we become disheartened and disillusioned.

This is when the voice of doubt can come again. The old self/ego takes advantage of our vulnerability in more subtle ways to bring us back to 'reality'. It is a dangerous time for anyone aspiring to become an angel as I found out today when that horrible voice returned.

"You're stumbling all the time: one minute you're confident, the next you are frightened; one minute you're enthusiastic, the next you feel hopeless; in the morning content, by evening complaining; on Monday joyful, by Wednesday moody; you fluctuate so much. Just watching you makes me dizzy!

Are these the steps of God's apprentice? Apprentice to the Almighty? The Truth? The Power? Have you got the right God? Maybe you have got the wrong apprenticeship? It's too big for you. Stop wasting time and return to normal life..."

I had to think about what the voice was saying because it was partly true. Still.

"I do stumble in many ways. I am learning and refining myself though. What you call 'normal' is just a return to the comfortable cage. No matter what, I will never return there. No matter what stumbling I have to endure, the cage is worse!

God has told me that stumbling and making mistakes is not a waste of time for an apprentice. Actually, it is a crucial part of transforming. Checking the consequence of my choices facilitates the changes necessary to manifest my potential, to fulfill my destiny."

"Destiny! Destiny! What is destiny? Another delusion. I will tell you straight what our common destiny is, so don't become so exclusive and make yourself out as something special. Our destiny is: to eat, drink, sleep, endure, express and die. That's our destiny! You think the destiny you are talking about is more elevated. Something extraordinary, beyond anything we can imagine."

As I listened to the voice, I wondered if it is really possible to become an angel.

"Reality is out there, not inside. This is your biggest stumbling block. Now understand the true points of reference; throw away that compass, burn that map and your destination of perfection. Purity and love is the usual absurd hallucination of those who attempt the impossible."

As the voice droned on, I wondered why I had these subtle fears and doubts. At the moment I didn't feel God or my destiny so strongly.

Suddenly I saw Lady Aditi appear in her dark blue-green robes, her eyes shining. She said, "Michael, the Great Lord has sent me to guide you a little. Be careful what you choose to hear; have some discernment."

Then I knew what to say.

"I trust the Great Lord. He is real and His knowledge will be my compass. Faith is stronger than your logic; it protects me against doubt."

But the voice echoed in my head, "Let's see, let's see how far you go until your next stumbling."

THE POWER OF FAITH

Faith is the merging of understanding, acceptance and experience.

Faith creates the inspiration to give ourselves completely: to belong to the One and to create a feeling of belonging in others.
This is my purpose, the task for which I exist
Acceptance facilitates steadfast commitment

Experience is the greatest stabiliser
It brings confident tranquility to the soul
It anchors our feelings and our thoughts
It creates a focus of love that remains stable
No matter what waves or storms come from the self
Or from others
Faith creates the capacity to
Feel the reality of the miraculous

Open the third eye
See beyond the borders of "How?" "What?" and "Why?"
Intuitively know that "this is the way"

Even if the way is not wholly clear or logical

Faith creates the capacity for trust
When I trust myself, I free myself from any limitation
When I trust God, I gaze on eternity
I feel humanity is truly a family where all belong -
God, angels, religions, cultures and people

"Belonging" echoes in the thoughts of all angels
The hearts of angels have no borders
They are filled with an unlimited faith in what humanity is
and can be.

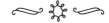

Pause for Reflection

How much faith do you have?

What is your faith based on?

*What experience or understanding do you
need to deepen your faith?*

SELF MASTERY

It is said that 'Mastery is not granted. It is earned'.

I now understood that becoming an angel requires a major and permanent shift in my consciousness.

A number of requirements are necessary for this transformation to take place, including practicing the following six important ways of living and being:

Cleanliness: a selfless agenda

The emerging master must be in the complete service of God, available and willing to serve moment by moment in honour of the sacred task.

Neutrality: not being pulled by anything or anyone knowing that all are equal

True justice can only be administered through neutrality. That is why angels are beyond nationality, religion and culture and why, although they work within many of these systems, they remain universal.

Stability: no event or person shakes the master

This anchoring is required most in chaotic situations, when combinations of fear and anger destroy order and balance. The master always observes the self to ensure that no spark, no trace, no speck of negativity finds a space to settle.

Compassion: this is given to everyone according to Divine Ordinance

The basis of this is detachment – that small space between the self and the other. Detachment makes feelings of compassion democratic, so that they never become stuck to a specific place or single person.

Constancy: the sign of being a true well-wisher

A flow of good wishes and pure feelings and comfort beyond what a person can comprehend, or accept, at a single moment is a sign of constancy. Masters allow everything to happen in its own time and keep thoughts of goodness flowing, rather than switching them on and off because of judgments.

Introspection: the breath of angelic life

However far an apprentice progresses – and even as he or she transforms into an angel – mastery is kept alive by remaining aware of the connection between the self and God.

If for any reason this connection is broken, lost or forgotten, the light short-circuits and darkness returns.

The angelic flight stops and consciousness, caught by gravity, falls into an abyss of habit. The fall can be so bad that the apprentice returns to what he was before, sleeping trapped in wrong identities, habits and routines. In other words, the angel is sent back to hell!

Constant introspection is the key to becoming and remaining an angel.

Without introspection the balance between reaching in and reaching out cannot function.

The angel – or spiritual teacher, saint or hero – must remain on *constant alert* because while serving on earth it is easy to be influenced by our old human nature, with its attraction to comfort and being governed by the senses.

Only introspection creates the state of alertness and attentiveness that protects the integrity of the server and the task.

Discernment, restraint, discretion and joy are the components of the inner checking that lead to permanent mastery.

When checking is positive we suffer no phobia, or guilt about our limitations. We build confidence and trust in our personal potential and this trust creates joy.

Joy motivates our quest for accomplishment and encourages us to celebrate our inner kingship.

Pause for Reflection

How do these statements resonate with you?
Which one(s) would you like to bring into your life? How?

SILENCE

We need the power to remain silent. We receive power by remaining silent. The power we receive from silence brings love and love makes us like angels.
Dadi Janki

Today we studied the power of silence. Lady Aditi says that silence is the language of angels. It is the method through which angels communicate with God. She says we must really want silence but…

How can I know silence?
How can I be silent?
How can I practice or experience it if I don't understand it properly?

Not talking. Is that it?
Not thinking. Is that it?
My mind refuses to remain still
Does it not like peace?
When I sit in silence

It feels as if insects scurry into my mind
Sometimes like cunning cockroaches that soil my clarity
Sometimes like ravenous worms that drill into my resolve
Sometimes like vengeful wasps that sting my faith

Lady Aditi says we must start from a point of inner stillness. Speak every word, think every thought, carry out every action with *complete attention*.

We must create a fresh quietness and never consent to the many plausible excuses that allow us to fill emptiness with the usual din and clamour of life.

We must
Observe more
Speak less
Think before thinking
Wait
Allow stillness to emerge
Stop binging on emotions.

Meditation (3)

I am determined
To pay full attention
No margin
No distraction

Remembering the origins of self
Remembering only the One
With all my mind
With all my heart
I am absorbed
Concentrated

In this state of being
I feel at one with the One
Connected
Tuned in

This transformative silence generates peace
In peace I can
Discern
Be clear
Learn
Change

THE TREASURES OF SILENCE

Today we were asked to write down the benefits of practicing silence. Here is my list. It is quite amazing. I never realised until now just how much it has helped me.

Silence humbles arrogance into silence

Silence neutralises the urge to defend myself

In silence I learn to speak through my eyes

Silence ends confusion

Silence guides me to the sacred point inside

Silence blesses the soul with awareness

Silence facilitates God's flow of power

Silence heals the mess created by extremes

Silence allows me to acknowledge impurity and transform it with love

One who perfects the art of Silence is known as a Silentist

The impossible is only possible for a Silentist

Here at the school we are all training to become 'Silentists'.
Great!

Pause for Reflection

What is your relationship with silence?
What could silence do for you?
How can you bring more silence into your daily life?

ABOUT TIME

Time is the moving image of eternity.

Plato

My ideas about time have changed completely since coming here. I used to think that time was linear, that it had a definite beginning and a finite end. This used to worry me because I could see things going from bad to worse around me and there seemed no real hope of things getting better, only ending in a horrible mess.

Now thanks to the knowledge shared by the Great Lord and Lady Aditi, I see time in a different way. Time is cyclical, just like the cycle of the seasons, or the life of plants, or the rotation of the planets round the sun. We are living through a special time.

Pause for Reflection

What makes this particular time on earth so special?

NOW IS THE TIME

Time has the capacity to heal
It gives us the opportunity to learn, change and discover
It dilutes the wounds of the past
It always signals, "Live in the Now"

Time measures the rhythm of life
There is a beginning, middle and end to
Each hour
Each day
Each life
Each epoch
Each cycle

Now we are living at the point of the end
And of the beginning

It is the time of the great change
The point of eternal intersection
Between the old and the new

It is at this time that God creates angels
The beings who partner with Him to

Bring peace and hope to humanity and
Facilitate the great return and the eternal beginning

At the moment of greatest darkness
The Eternal Pure Light comes
Creating:
Order from chaos
Balance from extremes
Belonging from isolation
Wisdom from ignorance
Respect from violence
Integrity from corruption

God creates the bridge
Humanity and Mother Earth cross back
To their original freedom and dignity

THE RHYTHM OF ETERNITY

My meditation experience is getting better and better because I am going deeper and deeper. I feel connected to eternity in a way I never thought possible.

I put my ear to the heart of time
I heard in His hands eternity rhyme
Moment by moment
Breath by breath
All was repeated
Each birth and death
Moment by moment
Wheel by wheel
Forever repeating
Necessity's zeal

THE SACRED SECOND

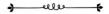

If I wish to become an angel, I need to become the master of time and the master of my thoughts. When time and thoughts are combined in a positive way, magic happens!

Here is a summary of today's lesson about time.

A second is the unit of time, just as a thought is the basic unit of consciousness. A body has many cells, and so do time and consciousness. Whether we measure time in terms of eternity, ages, cycles, centuries, millennia, years, seasons, months, days, hours or minutes – the basic unit, or cell, remains the second. We may measure consciousness in terms of awareness, attitudes, feelings, behaviour, choices, aliveness, responses but the basic unit, or cell, is always a thought.

If these two basic units of time and consciousness are weak, then the whole of time and consciousness suffers.

Just as cancer begins in a single cell and spreads to others cells, so the same happens in human life as the infected seconds and thoughts spread.

Ultimately this results in emotional, mental and even physical disease in the human body and mind, since our conscious life is acted and expressed within and through time.

Time is closely linked to thoughts. Time is wasted when thoughts are wasteful. Then the day becomes diseased with stress, fear, doubt and other unhelpful emotions.

If this becomes a habit, we feel as if we have no time, or that life has passed us by. We feel a failure, unable to cope with the demands of today, surviving rather than thriving. We feel empty and overcome.

What is the therapy for such a state of consciousness? How can we heal ourselves?

We can begin by coming back to the basic unit of time – the second – and the basic unit of consciousness, a thought.

If we take one second, the tiniest unit of time, and one thought, the tiniest unit of consciousness, we can make them work together.

In order for this to happen, we must fully accept the understanding we gain by practising Meditation (4) (page 99). *Under no circumstances rush or make this meditation exercise routine.* Otherwise it just becomes a technique and will no longer be experiential. It is especially important to give quality time to this practice and not to rush it, no matter what reason we create to justify the hurrying.

We must focus on the self when dealing with these tiny units. One mistake will destroy the whole process.

The slower and more concentrated we become, the deeper the thought goes and then we can tap into the pure energy of the original self and release it into consciousness.

When we try this as a method, we will never again honestly be able to say that we don't have enough time. Every day we will have lots of time.

The apprentice who moves to angelhood must completely master these units of time until they become eternity. They must also master their thoughts so fully that thinking stops and there is only *awareness*.

Meditation (4)

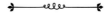

Take one second to think one thought
Slowly and faithfully think: "I am."
Add another second and another thought: "a soul"
Add another second or two and think: "I am peace"
Add another second or two and think: "I am a being of peace."

Repeat:
"I am a soul
I am peace
I am a being of peace."

Repeat these thoughts gently to yourself, paying special attention to them. There is no need to rush, no need for second thoughts or ideas going anywhere else. Just focus on these thoughts about the original self.

When this meditation in awareness is practiced properly – not as a technique, but as a heartfelt and accepted reality – pure new energy is released into the consciousness. A cleansing, or resurrection, takes place.

Throughout the day, gently but deeply repeat this one-second one thought meditative exercise. Each time may take 10, 12 or 14 seconds. This can be repeated, of course, so at one sitting you can build up the seconds of absolute concentration.

If you are naturally focused, you can continue for up to 60 seconds. Sixty seconds filled with 60 positive thoughts. This begins to heal and transform the self.

Repeating this meditation exercise in awareness often results in a tremendous release of energy, both inside and outside.

When concentrated for a long duration, let's say an hour or two, it results in an "atmic" explosion.

The word "atmic" derives from the Sanskrit word *atma*, which means "soul".

Unlike an atomic explosion, which is violent and destructive, an atmic explosion is a benevolent release of the purest energy of the human mind, which heals and harmonises people as well as nature and her elements.

When practiced at a collective level, the atmic explosion, which is subtle and invisible, restores the globe to its original order and balance.

How cool is that!!

Pause for Reflection

Do you consider time to be linear or cyclical?
What is your relationship with time?
How does your perception of time affect you and the way you
live your life?
Understanding the importance of this time, how could you
make best use of your time?

SPIRITUAL LOVE

According to Lady Aditi, spiritual love means never to become entangled in the threads of 'wanting'.

The more *attachments* we have, the more obstacles we will find thrown in our path.

Spiritual love inspires others to do and to be, to reach for something better in themselves and to manifest it to others as a selfless gift.

When we understand and experience that we are loved by God, we find ourselves and become inclusive.

Inclusiveness is both the flower and the proof of generosity – we no longer have to defend any frontiers. We no longer fear the unfamiliar.

To be inclusive we need to have fulfilled all our needs; such fulfillment creates a mature and contented state, which facilitates generosity.

Spiritual love simultaneously creates freedom and closeness, then no one or anything is put under obligation.

TRUE BELONGING

In this world which is so divided, it is so important to feel that we belong to something greater than ourselves.

We can never feel true belonging when we calculate, deceive or expect from others, or offer hooks camouflaged with promises that entice, trap and oblige.

Choice must be completely respected.

The power of our choice is stronger than what God can do for us.

God cannot trespass upon our choice. He respects our freedom.

When we feel respected by God, we gain a sense of belonging to the One who has given us space to be ourselves.

Belonging creates fulfillment, security and contentment.

Contentment is the proof of having honestly worked on the self.

It is the key foundation for an angelic apprenticeship.

Pause for Reflection

What does spiritual love mean to you?
How does spiritual love differ from other forms of love?
How could you be more loving?
Where do you feel you belong?
How could you increase your sense of belonging?

GRACE

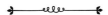

Lady Aditi says that grace is the magic ingredient that transforms everything.

Grace is God's power. It is non-human. Although received through human thought, it moves the mind and heart towards higher wisdom and love.

Grace can only come from God because only His being is unconditional.

I need God's grace to transform.

It is not enough just to make my own effort although that responsibility must be there.

Grace comes from the soul's vertical link to God
From conquering the intense gravity
Of a horizontal "give and take" existence

Grace is God's direct co-operation
Grace is a selfless, unconditional current of power that strengthens our:
Mind, making it serene

Will, making it determined
Intellect, making it humble
Feelings, making them clean

Grace is a gift given to the one who is honest with the self.

It is the spiritual alchemy that:
Dissolves the dirt in the mind and heart
Transforms mistakes into lessons
Creates the power to forgive the self
Makes the past truly past
Prevents remorse spoiling the best of today

Grace frees the Self from the self
It recreates and replenishes the soul

It can uplift, re-generate and cleanse because it comes directly
From God's Heart to my heart
From God's Mind to my mind

The only humans that attain this state of the unconditional are those who are transformed into angels. They do not need intercessors; they move directly via His love.

Now is the time for the direct flow of God's transformative love.

Grace is the key ingredient for metamorphosis
It opens the door to unlimited possibilities
Miracles become the norm

If I am careless, lazy or, especially, selfish, I cannot absorb God's grace when it is given. It is deflected.

Meditation (5)

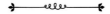

Become still, peaceful and serene.
Silently say to yourself the following words:

I become
I remember my essence
I return to my form as a point of light
I am a tiny, an infinitesimal point of very subtle energy

With a faithful and loving thought
I connect to the Eternal Point Source
The Benevolent Light

I am here now with You
Eternal Father and Mother Light

I am here
Connected
Receiving the current
Your Grace is in me working like silent alchemy
Releasing the angel within
And my destiny to serve

Pause for Reflection

What is the experience of God's grace?
What does a soul need to do to experience God's grace?
How can God's grace help me to change?
How can God's grace help the world to change?

SPIRITUALITY

Today we have been exploring the depths of spirituality. *It is the door through which we enter the world of angels.* Knowing that we are spiritual beings in a physical world is the foundation of everything we have been studying here for the past few years. Lady Aditi thinks we are now mature enough to understand that spirituality is both a science and an art.

Spirituality is a *science* because it requires understanding, learning and research.

Correct understanding is the basis of successful practice.

If our understanding is not right, then the result will not be either.

So, for better results we need to deepen our understanding through more research so that we can try again.

Otherwise we will go around in the same vicious cycle for a long time.

Only new research will bring about the new insight that breaks this gruelling spinning.

Spirituality is an *art* because it requires practice and exercise, that is, the refining of what we know theoretically.

When fully refined, spirituality becomes an art that inspires and uplifts others.

The perfected art is actually the way of being - like a pianist, or a dancer, or a poet who, after hours of thought and exercise, is able to express themselves with a precision and uniqueness that is appreciated.

Spirituality brings more than appreciation – trust emerges because there is coherence between the thoughts, words and actions of a spiritual person.

Where there is trust, relationships change and humanity and nature return to their original state of happiness and harmony.

This spiritual science and art form our wings, creating a movement upwards, the flight of liberation and service.

SPIRITUAL KNOWLEDGE

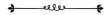

The proof that I am sincere about spiritual knowledge is that I use it.

It permeates all areas of my life. It is not a neat souvenir, something I can use to show off at particular times with particular people.

Knowledge is the seed of a new awareness

Silence waters that seed every day

Without silence there is no garden – all just remains potential.

Very often we speak of 'potentials' rather than 'realities' when we discuss spiritual ideas.

Pause for Reflection

What does 'spirituality' mean to you?

What have been significant moments on your spiritual journey?

HEALING

The years have passed so quickly. I can hardly remember the entire journey to this point, but I know I have something left to transform. I am no longer bothered by the doubt that Lady Maya throws at me. But there are brief moments when I feel empty.

I understand that it does not matter how much I know or do not know, I am a student of God. This feeling of apprenticeship protects me. It heals the mind of restlessness, the heart of selfishness and the intellect of arrogance.

The greatest healer is humility.

Humility means to see and go beyond the harsh, hard, brittle "I" - the "I" which blocks realisation and impedes those "Eureka" moments, which provide lifelines of enlightenment in a world plagued by uncertainty.

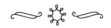

Pause for Reflection

What would you like to heal in your life?
What spiritual tools and insights from this book could help the healing process?

DISSOLVING GREED

When the mind is playing mischief even though the intellect has understanding, the conscience will not be able to see very clearly what it is that needs to happen.

Sister Jayanti

Lady Aditi asked me to write about my experience to share with the class. After a silent period this is what came to me:

When I feel empty I need to take –
From here and there
From this one and that one
I keep wanting more and more

In getting, I become possessive
Secure in what I have grasped and now own
I cry, "It's mine!"
Possessing and possessing gradually becomes obsessive
I must have
I must own
In order to exist
I become addicted

I lose my sense
My balance
My dignity

I realize I must wake up
I cannot go on like this

Where is my freedom?
Where is my happiness?
Where am I?

I must know myself and master myself

I must go beyond this illusionary me and find the original me

In silence and through Divine care I am gradually released

I discard the huge variety of masks that hide my great fragility

I watch with wonder

Divine love transforms my darkness into light
Helps me conquer the fabricated self.

Pause for Reflection

What are your addictions, great and small?
When you feel empty how do you fill the emptiness?
How could you use God to fill you instead?

ETERNITY AND HOME

The Great Lord came today and spoke to us about eternity.
He reminded us that we are all eternal beings of light.

In the world of eternity

All is Still
All is Silent
All is Changeless

The pure remains pure
The good remains good

Love remains love
It does not devolve into attachment

Truth remains truth
It does not devolve into dogma

The complete remains complete
It does not devolve into greed and need

Contentment remains content
It does not devolve into complaint and comparison

Peace remains peace –
It does not devolve into violence and justification

Only God remains as He is eternally

He is Constant Benevolence
There is no devolution
His home is eternity

My original home too is eternity
My being is natural, pure and free

Traveling into the world of time, expression and action
I gradually lost that original state of goodness

In a single moment
Through the silent journey of Thought
Through the window of Time
I often travel home throughout the day

If I do this often and deeply
I return to my original state of completion

When I am stable in this state of pure being
There are no strings and no shadows

God asks me to serve
To become His lighthouse
His messenger
His bridge

Meditation (6)

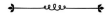

With one thought
One breath
One second
One heartbeat
I return to eternity

In this moment
I become tiny
Infinitesimal
I am essence
A point of light in eternity

I find
Serenity
Liberation and
My Eternal Partner
God

Beyond
The mechanics of matter
The grasp of time
The clutter of sound

The limits of breath
I experience the original goodness of self

All this happens
Through a moment
Through a thought

By gathering these moments of eternity every day
Silence can speak luminously through my eyes
Like a lighthouse, they guide others to peace and to God.

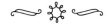

Pause for Reflection

What is the benefit of contemplating eternity?
Imagine what it would be like to experience
yourself as eternal?

STRENGTH, SHAKTI
AND ENERGY

Today the Great Lord revealed more about His power and how we can use it to bring about transformation.

Strength is the capacity to develop a talent, a virtue, a value.

When lived, these talents and virtues become my strength

Shakti is direct power from God – with nothing and no one in between.

Shakti is like grace - it enables miracles to happen
The impossible becomes possible
Wonders transpire that enhance life.

Energy is the ability to carry out and complete a task.

It is the positive force that is created and sustained from pure motives and will.

Such creative and constructive energy requires economy - not the waste of unnecessary thoughts, words and actions. Through such spiritual economy generosity is created - pure qualities are accumulated and radiated into souls, nature and time.

BECOMING GOD'S COMPANION

I have become God's companion. It is all I have wanted for so long, but now I feel it so clearly.

Friendship
I can be open to my heart's content with You
I can communicate without hesitation because I trust You
This is the original friendship in which, the human heart meets the Divine Heart and human thoughts meet Divine Thought
There is no need to speak
Being absorbed in this remembrance
I feel I have found what I have been searching for.

Relationship
I have found my other half
My eternal complement in You
I feel the bliss of immortal union
This oneness with God inspires me to change absolutely
I become truly genuine and worthy of this partnership.
Partnership

Partnership

Sharing the task of renaissance at this time
I am a partner of the Divine Director
He recreates the original play of life
My soul receives wings with which to fly and serve

As a partner I am a true trustee
I never become attached to the task
I am simply an instrument
A channel of God's light
God acts and I observe

I am a corporeal angel
Living at the intersection of time and eternity
Available to both God and humanity
No trace of darkness can ever threaten or penetrate me.

ANOTHER CHALLENGE

Today Lady Aditi told me that I had passed all the tests and that I am now officially an angel!

I am so pleased and grateful. Through all the trails and doubts, I have learned so much about myself and I am ready to face the future, whatever it may bring. God has given me the strength, understanding and ability to act as His instrument wherever and whenever He chooses..

However, I also know that ego will never stop trying to bring me down. Even today, of all days, it did its best to spoil things.

"Well done, Michael, I never have thought you had it in you.

Now you have so much power, so much knowledge, so many connections in high places. I am impressed! Let's discuss your options."

"I don't have 'options'," I replied. "My only desire is to serve humanity and be an instrument of God's peace and love. This is what the Great Lord has asked of me and I am very happy to do it. I have received priceless gifts and I wish to share them. Besides I could never have reached where I am now if it were not for God. I feel genuine gratitude. Without His blessings I could never have managed."

"God did nothing. *You* did all the work. He would not even exist if it were not for people like you who need to believe in Him. And as for blessings! They're just a bait, to make you subservient. You are so naïve and stupid. I can't believe you are content to be a mere servant! With your new radiant personality, you can have anything you want – fame, wealth, women, everything the world has to offer. Don't be a fool and turn your nose up at it.

And as for humility, forget that. It's just a psychological camouflage for servility. Don't be a server or an instrument. It's pointless. No one will thank you for it. Believe me, people are so ungrateful!

Be a leader, be a master. Enjoy yourself! Don't waste your time and energy on misplaced faith, dreams and speculation. Remember, you are just a human being like the rest of them and no amount of blessings, wings or halos can change that...

Where are you going? Come back here! Don't be such a fool, come back...Listen to me. Just listen!"

THE FINAL STAGE

Lady Aditi called me to her this morning. She said.

"Illusion has tested you well
Now look in the mirror
Be silent
Concentrate deeply
See
Do not be blinded by your eyes – really see."

As I gazed in the mirror, the "I" that I knew as Michael disappeared. I saw a being of light, so radiant, speaking to many, many people through the eyes; traveling here and there according to need, with wings, not feet, and healing just by touching the heart.

Lady Aditi continued, "This is your destiny. Deep inside, you have always known it. The Great Lord came just to remind you. He did the same to me a long time ago.

Always stay in this awareness. Do not go back to sleep under any circumstances. Do not be influenced by the cleverness of so called truths or reality, which are based on seeing, touching and hearing things in this physical world.

Truth is invisible; truth is subtle.

Remain awake, then thought and faith and time and God will work wonders through you."

Suddenly the room was filled with light and the Great Lord appeared. We embraced. I looked into His eyes and saw the reflection of an angel.

Pause for Reflection

What have you learned from Michael's journal?
What is the next step in your journey?
In what way(s) will you follow Michael's example
and become an angel?

MICHAEL'S STORY

PART II

THE GREATEST QUEST

It is love alone that gives worth to all things.

St Theresa of Avila

The last white petal fell from the rose fourteen years after Michael had come to Lady Aditi's school. It was 1915 and Michael was now nearly 28 years old. He could hardly believe that so many years had passed.

When Lady Aditi told him he was ready to leave and embraced him, he felt fourteen years old again, as he had been when he came to her school tucked away on that little road in Pietrasanta.

"Michael, you are now ready to complete the Greatest Quest. Here are eight areas of service. Find the 'greatest' among them and do whatever is necessary, whether it is for yourself or for others. Then and only then will you be equipped as an angel to go anywhere according to the call of time."

1 The Greatest Kindness

2 The Greatest Sorrow

3 The Greatest Resentment

4 The Greatest Waste

5 The Greatest Deception

6 The Greatest Barrier

7 The Greatest Need

8 The Greatest Compassion

As he walked back to the inn, Michael remembered her parting words and wondered how he would find them.

The Greatest Kindness

Sitting pensively on his bed in the attic room, Michael stared out the huge window, thinking of his eight tasks. The stars glittered like pieces of polished silver in the ebony sky. He knew he had to say goodbye to Signor and Signora Bianci.

They had allowed him to stay free of charge for fourteen

years, without even asking where he went so early each morning. As he thought of them, Michael knew that this was the greatest kindness he had encountered since his parents had died. His heart filled with gratitude.

Signora Bianci always made sure the food was to his liking and cooked sweets that would please him. Signor Bianci trusted him with the accounts of the inn and, by the age of twenty, Michael was supervising the staff.

Signor and Signora Bianci were growing old and Michael felt sad to leave them. As he thought of their kindness, his mind returned to his greatest sorrow – the death of his parents – and his greatest resentment, towards his grandmother and uncle. He knew that before he could embark on his task to serve as an angel he had to overcome these challenges.

He left his room to announce his departure. He found Signora Bianci knitting in her wooden armchair and Signor Bianci reading the paper by her side.

"This war is horrible. Such a waste of young life and for what?" said Signor Bianci, looking up from his paper as Michael approached.

Signora Bianci put down her knitting. They both looked at Michael lovingly, as if he were their own son. Although he had grown in size, it was obvious to both of them that he had grown in wisdom and they saw the light shining from his eyes.

"Signor and Signora, I came to say that tomorrow I will be leaving. I have finished my apprenticeship and it is time to move on and start my work. I just want to say how grateful I am. You have shown me the greatest kindness. I do not know what to give or say in return."

They did not seem surprised. In fact they smiled more and Signora Bianci said, "Michael, we are so happy for you. You have worked so hard and honestly. You did not miss a day of this long study. Now you will take up the task of the Great Lord and help the desperate and the hopeless. This is the greatest return."

Michael was struck by amazement. How did they know about the Great Lord? He had never mentioned it.

"Lady Aditi told us that you have been the best student for centuries," Signor Bianci smiled with pride. "We will keep Sekhmet here. In your travels you will not be able to look after a cat. And who knows, maybe in the future another student will come who she will serve as she has served you."

Sekhmet looked up with her usual knowing gaze, curved her tail and sat beside Signora Bianci. She meowed and stretched. Her task done, she was now relaxed and appeared totally confident of Michael's safety.

Signor and Signora Bianci hugged him in turn and the old man spoke, "Whatever you learned from the greatest kindness you experienced here, share it with others. That's the only return the Great Lord wishes. He wanted you to believe in the reality of kindness. He brought you here – share this with all those you serve. We were so happy to be with you. This will always be your home and we will always be here."

They did not cry. In that moment Michael understood that where there is true kindness there are no tears, just deep joy that the other has found well-being.

He took out the blue-green emerald, the stone that emitted the power of new life. Its colour had been transmitted into his eyes. He gave the now-clear stone to Signor Bianci, saying, "I am sure Lady Aditi will fill it with her own colour and it will be useful for someone in the future."

He turned to Signora Bianci and gave her the scarlet book in which he had written all his aims, hopes and experiences over the past fourteen years.

When he first received it from Lady Aditi it had been a slim volume. As he needed new pages, one would appear and now the book was very thick. Although Lady Aditi never asked to see it, Michael knew that she was aware of every word he had written.

Signora Bianci opened a page and read, "Today, I will try again to let go of any doubt or fear in my heart. No matter what has happened in the past, I will trust. I do trust. And if I begin to doubt this, I will ask the Great Lord to help me. Without trust I cannot change."

"You have done that haven't you Michael?" Signora Bianci observed.

"Almost there," he replied meekly. Michael knew that though he had changed deeply, a slight lack of faith lingered. He had to go to the tomb of his parents and the house of his grandmother and uncle and find out if everything really had a reason for happening.

Signora Bianci smiled. "I will keep your journal and one day share it with another of Lady Aditi's students, although it is said that a soul like you comes along only every 5,000 years."

"Well, you have a long wait then!" Michael laughed.

"In eternity, it's just the blink of an eye," replied Signor Bianci.

Michael packed his few things in a small bag, lay on his bed and waited for the dawn. As the ivory light of the moon glowed on his face, he thought of his trip tomorrow to Fiesole, to his parents' grave. He knew The Great Lord would not want him to be poisoned by resentment, yet this is what he felt as he thought of seeing his grandmother and uncle again.

The next morning Michael hugged Signora and Signor Bianci and waved goodbye. As they waved back, he saw they were surrounded by white light. Who are these people? he wondered.

The Greatest Sorrow

Michael travelled towards Fiesole, both walking and flying. It was so early he could see the stars while the sky turned topaz. When he dared to look into the depths of his heart there was a corner where he still felt the loss of his beloved parents. He had avoided this deep pain during his years at the school. Now he must face it. Michael wondered whether an angel really could remove every trace of his earthly life.

Suddenly, as dawn spread her violet-gold hands across the horizon, Michael found himself in the churchyard at Fiesole standing over the grave of his parents. The spring light made the white roses near the grave sparkle. As he stood there and remembered his dear parents, tears flowed. His heart stung. Do angels cry? He wondered.

No matter how much he understood the eternity of the soul, he missed the embrace of his mother and father.

I have just started the task, thought Michael, and already sorrow will not leave me. Have I failed even before I have started? Has the Great Lord's knowledge left me when I need it most?

Lost in thought, Michael saw his parents appear in front of him, rushing to embrace him. They looked the same but were sparkling with light.

"We are so proud of you Michael, so proud," said his father. "We knew, no matter what anyone said, that you were special. Your pure heart was destined for a special task. We are so happy."

"Look at those wings, Luca, the green, gold and red – just like the paintings of Fra Angelico," his mother exclaimed.

"But... how can you be alive?" stammered Michael.

"Michael, what have you been learning from the Great Lord?" quipped his father. "Haven't you yet understood that our essence cannot be destroyed simply because the body dies? Remember your many lessons about eternity from Lady Aditi."

They are not dead, realised Michael.

"How do you know about the Great Lord and Lady Aditi?" exclaimed Michael.

They did not answer. As he watched them, Michael slowly experienced the reality of eternity: no one really dies. The soul comes and goes at its appointed time.

He didn't know how long he stayed with his parents, but they did not need to speak to each other. Just being in their presence was all he needed. This sacred conversation was wordless, real and eternal. The joy and love expressed through their eyes satisfied something in his heart.

In that moment his deep, painful wound was healed and the crushing burden of sorrow lifted. He felt a great freedom. His parents embraced him.

"Michael, start your task," advised his mother, "and remember the rhythm of eternity. There is no separation, just constant comings and goings. We will always meet at the right time. Do not miss us: we are always near you; you just cannot always see or hear us. Now the Great Lord is with you. His love and trust will always support you and you will carry His love and hope to many."

Michael thought that his mother had become very wise. He wondered whether she and his father had also been taking lessons from the Great Lord. In a second they disappeared.

As he gazed on their grave, Michael saw the roses and felt soothed by their immaculate whiteness. He felt no sense of abandonment. He could now fly faster and, he was sure, further. He did not belong just to Italy anymore; the world was his home and humanity his family.

He was just ready to fly off when he heard a great wailing. He turned around and a torrent of sorrow engulfed him. He saw a small group of weeping people: a mother, supported by a father, followed by brothers and sisters and many other relatives, all dressed in black.

They could not see Michael as he moved closer to look. A coffin was being lowered into a grave and a priest was saying prayers for the departed soul, a young woman. The parents and siblings were inconsolable despite what the priest said and the comfort the relatives tried to give.

Michael felt the greatest compassion he had ever experienced. It must be hell to lose the one you love the most. What an unbearable separation. How could he heal such wounds?

He asked the Great Lord 'What shall I do?"

"You do not have to do anything. Just appear and remember Me. Through your eyes and angelic form they will receive peace and hope and feel that God has heard them and is with them."

Michael appeared in front of the family, startling the mother. Her wailing stopped and she sobbed, "God has sent an angel for Octavia."

Michael said nothing but God's light and love cocooned the gathering. As the instrument of the Great Lord he observed the healing, benevolent light growing around them.

"A miracle," they cried.

 "An angel has come to take Octavia to God," cried the astonished priest.

Michael saw the spirit of Octavia in front of him. She could not break free of the invisible ties of her hysterical mother, or the desperate sorrow and pain of her father, brothers and sisters.

She was lost in confusion. She spoke, telling them that she was well, that her real self had not died, and that she needed to move towards her destiny but they could not hear her.

Their sorrow held her like a prisoner.

Michael tried to guide her to the Great Lord, but she could not move.

Michael spoke, "Octavia is well. She is not the body in that coffin. She is a soul. Her essence is eternal and for the moment she has been called by God. If you really love her, let her go."

Her sisters, brothers and father became quiet. Her mother continued to sob, but as Michael's light surrounded her, she realised that if she really loved her daughter she must let her go. She became peaceful. The cloud of misery dissolved and the family felt relief.

"The angel? The angel has gone…"

The Great Lord had often told Michael that once a task is done, an angel does not linger. As Michael flew to his next destination, he saw with relief that Octavia and her family were at peace.

The Greatest Resentment

As Michael's greatest sorrow, the twin wound of resentment surfaced. He wondered if his grandmother was still alive after all these years.

In a second, this thought carried him to her house. Dressed now in ordinary brown clothes, he knocked at the door. No one answered. He knocked again. The door opened and a screeching assailed him.

"Who is bothering us at this time? Who…?"

Before she could finish her sentence, his grandmother, Nonna Sybila, recognized Michael and screamed, "Malfatto. Quick, Malfatto…. It's that boy – that devil!"

His uncle came rushing to the door, alarmed by his mother's screams. He looked at Michael, saying, "Mother you should rest. This is not Michael, just a man who's lost his way and wants directions." He had not recognized his nephew.

"Don't you see… don't you see?" she continued to screech.

"See what?" asked uncle Malfatto.

Michael noticed that his uncle had mellowed with the years, but his grandmother remained as nasty as ever. Why had they rejected him after the death of his parents? Why had they been so unkind? Thoughts and feelings forgotten for so long started to spin in his mind. His angelic nature observed the turmoil and knew that soon it would dissolve.

His grandmother abruptly interrupted.

"It's that boy of Luca's and his wretched wife… his eyes have more magic in them than before. He is evil. I always knew that. I knew."

"Quiet," Malfatto retorted. His uncle looked at him closely

and slowly recognised him.

"Well, Michael, good to see you after so many years. Come inside." His uncle had lost his bad temper and anger it seemed.

"No! no!", screamed the grandmother, "He'll curse the house, like his mother before him. I told that brother of yours a thousand times not to marry that witch. Now don't *you* fall under her son's spell..."

Michael followed his uncle inside and they sat down while his grandmother stood in a corner seething.

"What are you doing here Michael?" asked his uncle.

"I have finished my apprenticeship now and I am traveling to find work. I was in the area and thought I'd drop by. I still remember the hills of Fiesole with its trees, springs and birds. I used to like the songs of the birds. I felt that sometimes they were giving me a message."

"It's funny you say that Michael, because I was listening to a bird's song yesterday. I think it was a swallow. It was trying to tell me something with its wings," continued his uncle.

"What was the message, Uncle?" asked Michael.

Nonna Sybila could stand it no longer, "Don't get influenced by this one, Malfatto. He's like his mother – full of tricks, full of lies. He is up to no good. That witch stole your brother, who was such a good son, such a treasure in our house."

Malfatto paid no attention, "The swallow was writing with her wings 'soon you will meet an angel who will help you to forget the past and forgive your mother. He will also show you that your brother has forgiven you."

In that moment, sitting in front of Michael, Malfatto could see how his mother had always preferred his brother. When he married against her wishes, she began a raging vendetta, turning Malfatto against his own brother. He had been deceived.

"What are you two saying?" yelled his mother.

"Michael, somehow you seem different from when you were a boy. It's not just that you are older. The air around you is different."

Suddenly Uncle Malfatto opened his heart and shared with Michael, "Do you think your father can forgive me? I did not treat him well, nor your mother."

Michael was moved by his uncle's sincerity and embraced him saying, "I forgive you and I am sure my parents do, too."

At that moment Michael's resentment and Malfatto's guilt shattered like glass leaving them both free.

Turning to his grandmother, Michael was filled with compassion when he understood the underlying reason for her behavior. She had been obsessively possessive of her son. Losing him in marriage to a woman she so disliked, filled her with such great fury and bitterness that she lost her peace of mind and then her sanity.

The Greatest Waste

"Mother, look at Michael; his eyes are full of light."

She screeched and approached Michael with her frail fists in the air ready to strike him. As she approached, Michael realised this must be the greatest waste for any human being: to keep resentment inside, destroying all peace of mind and perspective. He realised that he could now let go of his angry feelings and the heavy burden of the past lifted from him.

Uncle Malfatto took his mother's arms and though she kicked and screamed, he held her back.

"Michael," he said, "Come in and stay the night."

Michael appreciated the thought and said, "Thanks, Uncle, but I have to go."

"Go where? It's dark; you'll lose your way."

"No he won't," hissed his grandmother, "the devil has eyes to see in the dark."

Michael waved goodbye and literally flew to his next challenge. Now with his thoughts freer and more powerful, he could fly anywhere.

The Greatest Deception

It was 1915 and the Great War had begun. They called it "the war to end all wars." It had to do with land, territories and injustice, they said. Lady Aditi had told him that war was the result of greed, fear, lack of respect and desire for power and position.

He himself did not know much about it – he had been busy with another silent war for fourteen years. An inner battle for self-mastery in which he had had to overcome inner voices of deception and stop depending on others and expecting things from them which they could not give.

He also had had to fight disappointment and the resentment when others' behaviour was not to his liking and, possibly the greatest deception of all, subtle arrogance. The Great Lord described it as an attachment to the self that does not allow one to fully respect another.

Michael remembered a more serious deception, which he had not shared with anyone. He understood later that this was the greatest deception of all: the desire for power and position, a self-satisfied feeling of dominance over others through well-argued ideas. He had never mentioned it to Lady Aditi or the Great Lord but felt sure they knew.

It had taken him some time but he realised that no matter what he learned and no matter what he became, his allegiance must always be to the task of the Great Lord and those he served.

Michael remembered Lady Aditi's words, "Always we are students, no matter how high we fly, how wise we become, how much others may be impressed by us, we must remain sincere to the task – or we pollute both the self and the task."

Michael knew he had to keep a constant connection with the Great Lord – he could see how just one thought coloured by human desire could tempt him to play the master and fall. He had to keep alert.

The Greatest Barrier

As he passed the silent monastery of St. Francis in Fiesole, Michael stopped to rest by the door. Dawn was breaking in her scarlet glory over the valley, the birds sang and a swallow brushed his cheek to wake him. It was as though she knew he needed to move on.

Michael lay to rest for a few moments but fell into a deep sleep. He dreamed of a huge army of soldiers lying dying and wounded, shooting and shouting. Amid the desperation and fear the soldiers raised questions about honour, glory, freedom and gallantry.

As he watched the immense chaos, the Great Lord came to him. Though He was not physically visible, Michael felt His voice speaking through his thoughts and saw an orb of light.

"Michael, go to the place where there has been so many wars and so much sorrow; help them conquer the greatest barrier and fulfill their greatest need."

Michael awoke to find himself in the midst of the war that Signor Bianci had been reading about in the newspaper. He saw small boats filled with thousands of soldiers heading to shore. The soldiers held their guns ready. Up in the hills crouched other soldiers, dressed differently but otherwise the same, firing down on the boats as they landed and the soldiers disembarked. It was a chaos of orders, machine-gun fire, shouts, explosions and cries; bodies lay everywhere, blown apart, disfigured. For a second Michael thought he had reached hell.

I have been in school too long, he thought. How can humans do such things to each other? Is it possible? What can I do? Where do I start?

As he stood above the earth the moans of the wounded reached him from the shore and the hills. Some shouted, "For King and Country" and others shouted "Victory." He thought he also heard the words "Freedom" and "Allah."

As their faces came into view he saw that they were from many countries – England, France, Germany, Turkey and even Australia and New Zealand. The bloom of each country's youth was bullet-ridden or blown away by grenades. He did not know what to do.

As he wondered the Great Lord came, invisible but for an orb of light.

"Michael, you look confused!"

"Well, my Lord, who should I help? Who deserves it more? Who is the enemy?"

"Since you have become an angel, Michael, you can no longer think like a human. You see, the greatest barrier in the human race is their strange way of thinking. They presume that someone is right and someone is wrong, one side is just and the other unjust, that everyone is either friend or enemy. Humans always justify their actions and often resort to killing each other over such things. You know humans don't you, Michael?"

Michael remembered his human past and his tendency to label, justify and condemn without much thought.

"Michael, you have to help humans overcome this barrier of perception. If it were not so serious, it would be funny – they are so caught in their tiny worlds of pettiness and inflated self-importance. This breeds dogmatism and fanaticism, which in turn creates the next greatest need in humans... to be something, to show that they belong to the right race, the right religion, the right nationality, the right politics at any cost.

This need motivates so much of their violence. They try

to gain a sense of identity, value and belonging through this abstract "rightness." This attachment to role, country and nationality leads to a superiority complex which is catastrophic for their well-being and that of Mother Earth.

Michael, co-operate with them all… whether they believe in God or not, no matter what their religion, nationality or politics. Every single person has something right and something wrong within themselves; every country has justice and injustice within its system. The problem is that in the human world, truth is at very best partial. This is the greatest barrier they must break through."

The Greatest Need

The battle raged beneath Michael as he landed on a hill nearby. The Great Lord continued to speak.

"For the survival of humanity and Mother Earth, Michael, you must help them to overcome their greatest barrier. They can only do this when they fulfil their greatest need: to have the humility and respect to reclaim their inner peace and so bring about reconciliation.

Angels do not have borders in their heart. You are an angel now and will continue to be for eternity. As an angel you go beyond these differences. When you are in your original spiritual consciousness and connected to Me, you can give light to all, irrespective of their role or nationality.

Whether victim or oppressor, all need to learn and a drop of love and mercy will help them to see their own and each other's worth. When you give light to victims, they will recognize their value and not allow themselves to be misused. Giving light to those who oppress will make them more humane.

There are many things we could say, Michael. However, until this greatest barrier and need is removed, human consciousness will not change and such terrible conflicts will continue to repeat themselves."

"But, Great Lord, it is said that this is the 'war to end all wars'. Nothing can be worse than this… surely they will not make such mistakes again?"

"Michael, if the human race can learn, then certainly this violence will end. There are people who try very hard to bring this about. However, we will see what humanity actually learns. Whatever happens, Michael, always be available for them."

"Do you think I will have to do this task in future conflicts?"

"Michael, God does not think, He just sees. And you will see for yourself. But, for the moment, guide and support these soldiers."

The orb of light dissolved, leaving Michael among the dead, dying and struggling soldiers. He was not sure how to help them overcome their greatest barrier and greatest need. The task extended far beyond this battlefield. It had to be done elsewhere; could there be schools that taught such things; schools for people from every walk of life?

For the moment, he was here and must act here. Michael floated over hills and gullies, deciding to remain invisible and see what action would be appropriate.

Suddenly he heard a breathless moaning and came across a bleeding soldier sprawled on the ground. He was about 19 or 20 years of age and very badly injured but still conscious. The young man was speaking deliriously.

"Wrong... is it wrong what I feel now? My mates would say 'you've lost your courage'. Maybe... I can't help it... my mum, dad, brother, sis... I want to see them again. My friends... walk and talk with them again.

Maybe it's wrong but for me that's more important than heaven... if you are there God... if you exist... and listening... I just want to live, to be with them again. I'm lonely here, God... so lonely... I want to live... my mates think I'm dead 'cause no one is coming to search for me..."

As Michael looked at the badly damaged body, he knew it was not possible for the young soldier to live. He felt the youth's loneliness, his life blown apart. With a thought Michael made himself visible and, without speaking, he lifted the recruit over the ridge to where his companions would find the body.

The soldier was too tired to feel surprise but found great relief and comfort. His heart filled with peace as Michael carried him over the hill and he murmured, "God, you do exist. I know I will see them again."

His friends shouted, "Look, Dave's over there. How did he get there?"

They scurried, low to the ground to avoid sniper's bullets, to kneel beside him.

"How you doing Dave?" one of them asked. Dave could only smile at them.

"Look at his face, it's so peaceful. In this hell you would think he'd seen an angel."

With his last drop of energy Dave whispered, "I did."

As each day passed more graves were dug, more crosses went up and hopelessness quietly spread through the camps. Michael did what he could and, though they did not always see him, some soldiers felt his presence and knew they were no longer alone.

An English lieutenant nervously watched the Turkish trenches. The whole area was full of gullies. Flies and lice were climbing over his body. On the ship over, he and his companions had spoken of Odysseus, of Jason and of Achilles. They had seen themselves as a new band of Argonauts sailing forward on their quest.

On the battlefield, the romance and chivalry of schoolday Greek myths had left him quickly. The disillusioned lieutenant had lost his innocence as well as many of his friends - now the multi-headed dragon of bullet, shrapnel and dysentery had wiped out so many.

Facing the horror of war, the young lieutenant felt deceived by his commanders; they had not told the whole truth. No one who signed up had expected this kind of quest – the gas, the grenades, the artillery, the diseases, the maiming and the shock of easy defeat.

Suddenly, a Turkish soldier popped up from an opposite trench, holding his rifle steady for a few seconds face to face with the lieutenant. Then he fired. Immediately another gunshot sounded and the Turkish soldier crumpled to the ground.

As the lieutenant lay dying he saw Michael and gasped, "Are you Apollo?"

"Not exactly Dennis, but I am here to help you leave and go to your destination."

The lieutenant felt reassured to be called by name and with his last breath gasped, "Where am I going?"

Michael showed him an orb of light, saying, "Dennis, you are going home where you can rest."

And without any doubt, fear or hesitation Dennis left the

war-torn earth in great peace.

In the opposite trench Michael found a Turkish soldier praying, "*Allahu Akbar… Subhaana rabbiyal Alaa…*"

As he lay dying, Michael came closer and heard him repeating the same words over and over again. He struggled to speak, so Michael propped him up to breathe better.

As Michael looked at him, the man's deep brown eyes shone in recognition and hope. He grasped Michael's forearm and uttered more words, "Michael! Michael, please go to Alara… go to her and tell her Allah's will is absolute."

"Mehmet, I am not so sure this was Allah's will."

But Mehmet was not listening, "O Angel, please tell her that I love her and not to remain in pain for the rest of her life. She has to let go of her memories. I know her. She will remain obsessed with my death and ruin her life. She must let go and keep on living. Our children need her."

In a thought, Michael was in front of a woman. Her black hair was tucked neatly under a dark blue scarf and her green eyes were filled with sorrow. Her lips repeated the same words over and over; it seemed she was praying for someone.

Suddenly she looked up, and seeing Michael in his form of golden light, she shrieked, "No, please do not tell me, please! Mehmet is not dead, Mehmet is not…"

Michael kept silent. He stood still. Alara now knew. She

wept but kept her eyes on Michael. He remembered the Great Lord and from his eyes a great light shone on Alara. It embraced her and comforted her in her sorrow.

She felt a loneliness she had never known before and a wound that would never heal. From the wound came hate. She thought of these foreign people who had come to take her land and forced Mehmet into this bloodbath. Already she was becoming bitter.

She looked at Michael and asked for vengeance, pleading, "You have seen the injustice. They deserve to be punished for what they have done. Now my children are without their father. Those foreigners need to be punished. Please, ask God to do this for me."

As she spoke she saw Mehmet beside the angel. She rushed forward to touch him, but couldn't. Mehmet was made of light and her hand passed through him.

Mehmet softly spoke to her, "Alara, not like this; don't think like this…. You will waste your life and the lives of our children if you remain like this. Accept the will of Allah."

Alara in her usual headstrong manner, cried, "I can't accept it. I won't," and broke down weeping.

Deeply moved by his wife's sorrow but understanding her stubbornness, Mehmet continued, "Alara, we are all victims of something bigger than ourselves. We get deceived by ideas. There is no benefit in blame or revenge.

I was about to shoot a young English soldier and, as our faces met, I saw myself in his eyes and he saw himself in mine. He was as confused as I was; he felt as cheated as I did – but I had been told that he was my enemy. I shot him and he fell... and in that second I asked his forgiveness. What we were doing to each other was terrible. I know he felt the same. Hate achieves nothing."

Mehmet disappeared but Michael remained powerfully silent. Alara knew hate achieved nothing; how often had Mehmet told her so? But emotion does not make space for reason.

She gazed at Michael and his loving light gradually dissolved her bitterness. Slowly, Alara decided to let go and try to understand what Mehmet had told her about forgiveness. She had to trust life again and move on. Mehmet would have wished this for her. She was even more sure that this was what the Great Lord would wish for her.

Michael stayed with Alara long enough for her to become peaceful and then he returned to the battlefield where he saw more crosses, more graves, more bodies and disease. With all that wasted youth, Michael found it difficult to hold back the tears.

He had done so well until now but returning to the same carnage was just too much for his angelic heart to take. Couldn't the Great Lord have stopped all this? Why such death and destruction over a piece of land?

The Greatest Compassion

In his confusion, Michael had forgotten to follow the direction of Lady Aditi – just to be quiet and connect to the Great Lord. He had started to get sidetracked by all the sorrow he had witnessed.

Lady Aditi appeared in front of him as he sat among the quiet dead. When he saw her he said, "All this... so much despair."

A tear trickled down his cheek even as he remembered her direction, "Angels do not cry."

Before she could say anything Michael burst out, "I know! I know angels don't cry, so maybe I am not cut out for this job. Maybe I am a failure."

Lady Aditi looked at him with compassion, "Michael, you know this is not just a job. It's a precious task. Through it, hundreds of thousands can be helped; you're building a bridge for them and they will need it even more in the future."

Michael was shocked, "Do you mean – it can get worse than this?"

"If humanity does not learn from its mistakes and start to respect each other, then it is inevitable."

With this Lady Aditi left, knowing that Michael had understood and would succeed in his task.

For a moment, Michael went forward in time. He wished to see if humanity had learned some lessons. But no! He saw bigger bombs, deadlier warplanes and whole cities as battlefields. He saw weapons so sophisticated that countries could be destroyed in an instant. And nature, too, seemed to be in upheaval. Huge waves enveloped the earth; there were earthquakes toppling buildings and cyclones. Why was nature so angry? He did not want to see any more.

Then he saw himself and many other apprentices who had been transformed into angels circling the globe. They were unaffected by the chaos, spreading light and comfort everywhere. He saw himself in that future and he knew that all this had to be but it would pass.

Moving further forward in time, he saw a beautiful garden filled with happy people. The earth had definitely changed from a place of war to one of complete peace. Something must have happened.

Suddenly the image grew dimmer and he returned to the present.

He knew then that this violent condition on earth would not last forever. That eventually human beings would come to realize that the only way to put an end to suffering would be to turn the rhetoric of humility and respect into a living reality.

Michael returned to the battlefield and found himself

cradling a dying Indian soldier, gasping, "*Om Namah Shivaya, Om Namah Shivaya… Har har Mahadev.*"

Unlike the other dying soldiers, he was calm. He clearly saw Michael and did not seem surprised, saying, "Divine being, you have been sent because I know my time has come. My soul will leave this costume of clay and come again, according to the actions I have performed. All is happening as it should."

Michael just looked at him. As the soldier chanted, "*Om Namah Shiva…*" an orb of light appeared. The light embraced him as his soul left. There was no fear; he moved towards a destination he somehow knew and felt at ease. In silence, and with a smile, he thanked Michael and moved on.

Michael had learned a great deal and now knew what to do.

As the crosses and graves increased day after day for eight more months, he travelled over the hills, guiding thousands of soldiers who needed his assistance. Many knew and felt eternity; others were not so sure, but when they experienced the light of the Great Lord they felt freedom and comfort. It was not a matter of belief, but of experience. Michael noticed that no matter what the soldier's faith, all experienced the benevolence of the Light.

From that day for as long as he was needed, he would serve in his uniform of light, becoming a living lighthouse recognised and trusted by all those in need.

ABOUT ANTHONY STRANO
1951 - 2014

"And see, no longer blinded by our eyes."
Rupert Brooke

Anthony was born in Australia of Italian parents and grew up on a farm where he developed a deep love and respect for nature.

In his early twenties, he set off to travel the world and eventually found himself high in the Aravali mountains of Rajasthan, North-West India, where he discovered the Brahma Kumaris and Raja Yoga meditation.

From then on Anthony's life was dedicated to developing a deep, loving relationship with the One, transforming himself and serving humanity. He became a much sought after spiritual teacher, speaker, author and mentor sharing his practical experiences and understanding of God in a very accessible way.

During his life Anthony travelled to more than 50 countries and touched many people through his simplicity, humility, authenticity, humour and joy in living.

Anthony took a keen interest in the mythology and sculpture of ancient Greece. He delighted in the angelic images to be found in Italian Renaissance art. He was deeply touched by the poetry of the English poet Rupert Brooke and very moved by the senseless slaughter of so many young men in the First World War.

Anthony was a prolific author and writer of articles (including a blog for the Huffington Post) and a number of his lectures and meditation commentaries were recorded and produced as CDs. See bibliography.

As the Director of the activities of the Brahma Kumaris in Greece, Hungary, Cyprus and Bulgaria, he was an inspiration.

Over the years he also co-coordinated five Science Symposia on "Science and Consciousness" in Greece and Mexico and also Arts Symposia and retreats in Italy, Spain and Greece.

Anthony passed on suddenly in Brazil during a lecture tour.

A moving tribute to him can be found on Youtube along with a beautiful video called '18 Steps From Human To Angel'

ABOUT BRAHMA KUMARIS

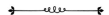

The Brahma Kumaris is a network of organisations in over 100 countries, with its spiritual headquarters in Mt Abu, India. The University works at all levels of society for positive change.

Acknowledging the intrinsic worth and goodness of the inner self, the University teaches a practical method of meditation that helps people to cultivate their inner strengths and values.

The University also offers courses and seminars in such topics as positive thinking, overcoming anger, stress relief and self-esteem, encouraging spirituality in daily life. This spiritual approach is also brought into healthcare, social work, education, prisons and other community settings.

The University's Academy in Mount Abu, Rajasthan, India, offers individuals from all backgrounds a variety of life-long learning opportunities to help them recognise their inherent qualities and abilities in order to make the most of their lives.

All courses and activities are offered free of charge.

For more information visit:
www.brahmakumaris.org
www.inspiredstillness.com

SPIRITUAL HEADQUARTERS

PO Box No 2, Mount Abu
307501, Rajasthan, India
T: (+91) 2974-238261 to 68
F: (+91) 2974-238883
E: abu@bkivv.org

International Co-ordinating Office & Regional Office for Europe and The Middle East

Global Co-operation House,
65-69 Pound Lane,
London, NW10 2HH, UK
T: (+44) 20-8727-3350
F: (+44) 20-8727-3351
E: london@brahmakumaris.org

....

REGIONAL OFFICES

AFRICA

Global Museum for a Better
World, Maua Close,
Off Parklands Road, Westlands,
PO Box 123, Sarit Centre, Nairobi,
Kenya
Tel: (+254) 20-374-3572
Fax: (+254) 20-374-3885
E: nairobi@brahmakumaris.org

THE AMERICAS AND THE CARIBBEAN

Global Harmony House, 46 S.
Middle Neck Road,
Great Neck, NY 11021, USA
Tel: (+1) 516-773-0971
Fax: (+1) 516-773-0976
E: newyork@brahmakumaris.org

AUSTRALIA AND SOUTH EAST ASIA

181 First Ave, Five Dock,
Sydney, 2046
Australia
Tel: (+61) 2 9716-7066
E: ashfield@au.brahmakumaris.org

RUSSIA, CIS AND THE BALTIC COUNTRIES

2, Lobachika, Bldg. No. 2
Moscow – 107140, Russia
Tel: (+7): +7499 2646276
Fax: (+7) 495-261-3224
E: moscow@brahmakumaris.org

brahmakumarisru.com
spiritual-development.ru